CELEBRATE!
Your Festival Handbook

RAKHI & BHAI DOOJ!

CELEBRATE!
Your Festival Handbook
RAKHI & BHAI DOOJ!

hachette INDIA

First published in India 2011 by Hachette India
(Registered name: Hachette Book Publishing India Pvt Ltd)
An Hachette UK company
www.hachetteindia.com

SRD

ISBN 978-93-5009-310-8

Hachette Book Publishing India Pvt Ltd
612/614 (6th Floor), Time Tower,
M.G. Road, Sector 28, Gurgaon 122001, India

Typeset in Goudy Old Style 11.6/14.8 and Futura 10.5/15
by Eleven Arts, New Delhi

Printed and bound in India by
Manipal Technologies Limited, Manipal

Contents

Super Sibling Stories 1

1. The Writing on the Wall 3
   Roopa Pai
2. All about Big Brothers 17
   Anu Kumar
3. The Step Tapes 33
   Rituparna Chatterjee
4. The Henna Boys 45
   Deepa Agarwal
5. A Witch's Gift 55
   Ani Sengupta
6. The Tiger Man 64
   Retold by Kanika Sharma
7. Black Rain 71
   Raja SG
8. A Pinprick 78

All about Rakhi and Bhai Dooj 85
Subhamoy Das

1. Rakhi: The Thread of Love 87
2. Rakhi Legends from Hindu Mythology 89
3. Rakhi Tales from Indian History 92
4. Bhai Dooj: The Post-Diwali Festival 94

Fun Festival Activities 97

- Make your own *rakhi*
- Safety Pin *rakhi*
- String *rakhi*
- Prepare a Rakhi Ceremony
- Pocket Wall Hanging
- The Story of your Lives
- Spanish Giant Paper Mask
- Photo Project
- Stop-Motion Animation
- Pick-Up-Sticks
- It's a Line-Up
- The Great Rakhi Match-Up
- Who Am I?
- Wish like an Egyptian
- String Pictures
- Get a Picnic Together
- Staircase

- Battleships
- Limerick your Gift
- Pillow Pack
- Milk Barfi
- Make your own Mithai
- Sandesh
- Family Tree

Festivals Rock! Diary 123

Your Festival Playlist 129

1. Rakhi and Bhai Dooj Super Songlist! 130
2. Festival Movie Marathon! 131

Notes on the Contributors 133

Super Sibling Stories

The Writing on the Wall

Roopa Pai

I had won it! I had actually won it! And not some two-bit 'Honourable Mention' either (Yuck! I totally hated it when that happened! As if there was any *honour* in losing!). No-oh *sir*—the big fat trophy pressing into my spine through my backpack proved it. I had just been crowned—*wa-ai-it* for it—Absolute-and-Undisputed Champion at the inter-school Robotics Challenge—*yessssss*! I had wanted this so much, not just for myself but for Mia and Dandy too. They would be so pleased, so proud.

Apparently, it was the 'first time in the history of the Challenge' that a *girl* had won it, so the organizers were going slightly nuts. 'Like the Challenge is a hundred years old or something,' snorted Nushki, my best friend, 'instead of a measly five.' She didn't mean to take away from my victory—no, that wasn't it at all—Nushki just had this really strong feminist streak, and people acting all disbelieving and awed because a girl had won a science challenge *really* got her mad.

I was cool about stuff like that, though. My family was full of aunts and girl cousins who were science and math freaks. My big brother Anish would be 16 next month but I could cream him any day on any given topic covered in the eighth grade science curriculum, and then some. Guaranteed. So I never felt the need to prove that girls were as good as boys at science—I *knew* they were.

Plus, I didn't really care what other people said, about *anything*. Most of the time, anyway. If people began saying things that upset me, I just whipped out my invisible noise-cancelling headphones and clapped them on. It was like watching TV with the volume off—suddenly, all of them looked like complete morons, flapping their arms around and pulling weird faces. It was seriously funny—I had to make a real effort not to giggle.

Mia and Dandy, my brilliant scientist parents, thought it was I who looked moronic—eyes glazed, mouth half-open—when I did that headphones thing. They worked on cutting-edge research in mechatronics and other fancy-sounding stuff like control engineering, nano-chemistry, cybernetics—but they never figured the simple things out, like the connection between the invisible headphones and the conversation around me.

'Snap out of it, Sushma,' Dandy would say irritably when he noticed I had my headphones on. 'Earth to Sushi!' Mia would say, the very next second. 'Come in, Sushi!' It was supposed to be a joke, so I would smile as I took my headphones off, but seriously, a joke sort of loses its zing when you've heard it 23,545,301 times . . .

Oh, in case you're wondering, Mia is short for *Mamma Mia*—my parents had worked for a year in a scientific institute in Rome when Anish was little, and apparently, he had loved hearing people say '*Mam-ma Mee-ya!*' there, and then Mom discovered that it actually meant 'my mother', and she thought it was just too cute and she tried to get him to call her that, but, as usual, he couldn't be bothered to take the trouble to say the whole thing, even to make her happy, so he shortened it to Mia, and Mia she became. I know, long story.

Dandy's story is simpler—my dad's name is Sandeep and everyone calls him Sandy and so I used to call him that too but my grandmom thought it was too rude and insisted I call him Daddy, so, as usual, I took the diplomatic way out and pleased both myself and my grandmom—somewhat—by calling him Dandy. He loved it, for some reason, so that's what *he* became.

Something familiar zipped past the window of the school bus. I snapped back to the present—my stop was almost here. Mia's little yellow car was parked in its usual place—hurray, she was home! She was always pleased when I won anything, but this one would be extra, extra special. I gathered up my things and headed for the exit. The doors opened, and I leaped off the bus.

Bad move. I am not a natural leaper—I am a shuffler. Actually, more of an ambler, a s-t-r-o-l-l-e-r. But I was so excited about the Robotics thing that I wasn't thinking straight. So I leaped, with the heavy trophy in my backpack weighing me down. The next second, *bam!* I had landed hard on my backside, legs splayed inelegantly in front of me, looking rather foolish.

'Nice one, Buttowski!' yelled the Jock, leaning out of the bus window as it sped off. 'Lucky you have all that adipose in the right place!' The boys guffawed. The girls tittered. I couldn't actually hear them—the bus was way down the road by then—but some stuff, you just *know*. Girls always laughed at the Jock's jokes, hoping like mad he'd notice them or something. I never laughed—my problem was that he noticed me rather too much.

If the Jock had read my thoughts, he'd probably have said, 'That's because there's so much *more* of you to notice, Buttowski!' and set the whole bus off again.

So now you know—I'm the Fat Girl with the Big Butt. There's one in every class.

But, of course, high-achieving me couldn't just be that—that would be too commonplace. So I was the Nerdy Fat Girl with the Big Butt—and trust me, that is *not* a killer combo when you're thirteen.

'Buttowski!' chortled a familiar voice. 'Bwahahahaha!'

I froze. What was Anish doing at home on a Tuesday afternoon? He was supposed to be at his new school—the liberal, *la di dah*, 'let it all hang out' school—where students boarded four days a week, returning home on weekeneds. Just FYI, this one was his fourth school—in as many years. I looked up warily, and noticed the second car in front of the house—Dandy's. This was not good. It could only mean one thing—Anish was in trouble again.

I picked myself up and walked past him towards the house, my blood boiling. It just wasn't fair! My brother ruined my life on a daily basis, hogging my parents' mind-space even when he wasn't around, turning me into She-Who-Does-Not-Exist. But just this once, he could have given it a rest. Just for today, when I so totally deserved to have Mia and Dandy really *look* at me and listen to what I had to say.

'*Buttowski*!' he persisted, tossing his shoulder-length hair—yes, the liberal school allowed it—out of his eyes. 'Wish *I'd* thought of that one!'

The bile rose in my throat. 'Stop wishing already,' I said acidly. 'You couldn't come up with it in a million years if you tried—you don't have the brains.'

'Oh, I see. And the *Jock* does?' His slim, tall frame doubled up with silent laughter as I bit my tongue in consternation. Everyone knew I detested the Jock, and here I was, complimenting him for thinking up a rude name for me! Oh, well *done*, Sush.

But that was the effect my brother had on me. Two minutes in his exhilarating company and my mood had gone from whatever it had been before to black-as-thunder—my throat got tight, my head throbbed, my eyes stung, and Fat Nerdy Girl morphed into Fat Nerdy Girl with Ugly Scowly Expression who said Dumb Things. There was nothing I could do to control it. Even my trusty noise-cancelling headphones were a complete fail in this situation.

'So what happened this time, bro?' I said, feeling an extra dose of meanness shoot into my bloodstream. 'Did they kick you out because you were a) too violent, b) too dumb, c) too offensive, d) all of the above?'

'Tch, tch, tch,' Anish slouched along beside me, his hands tucked deep into the pockets of his way, wa-ay-y low-slung jeans. 'So much anger in one so young. I worry about you, Grumpy—you've got to lighten up.' He glanced at me, frowning. If I didn't know him as well as I did, I would have thought he was actually concerned. But he wasn't finished. 'No wonder you have no friends!'

Effortlessly, my brother had hit a weak spot once again. Nothing surprising about that of course—he had had years of practice. The worst part was, I had never had a good comeback to this one. Until now. 'I do too!' I yelled triumphantly. 'I have 157 friends on Facebook!'

My brother stared at me, disbelieving. I felt a warm, smug glow—chew on *that*, bro. Come to think of it, he probably didn't even *know* I was on Facebook—I certainly hadn't bothered to tell him. I hoped that hurt—knowing he was not one of the 157. Then he began to laugh. He *roared* with laughter. It unnerved me a little.

'What?' I demanded through clenched teeth. 'What is so funny?'

'157 friends,' he shook his head. '*That's* funny. So . . . so . . . you check who's online, and go "wassup", and they go "nm—nothing much", and you go "wat u doing" and they go "nm" again, and then, suddenly, they go "gtg" and you say "bye". And you think "Wow. I just had a conversation. That's what friends do, don't they? They have conversations." And you feel like a regular Ms Popular,' he stopped, and guffawed again. 'Sucker.'

My eyes prickled with tears. I ran through the front door and dashed up the stairs to my room, my backpack bouncing painfully against my spine. Why was my brother so mean? What had I ever done to him? I chucked my backpack, trophy and all, hard against the wall, slammed the door, and threw myself on the bed, sobbing.

'Sush!' Mia's voice sounded strained. 'Come on down—your tea is ready.' Not bad, Mia, I hissed bitterly into the pillow. You actually realized I was home, even on a day such as this.

Directly below me, from Dandy's study, I could hear the hum of his voice, its volume and pitch steadily rising as he put Anish through the 'when will you grow up blah blah . . . High time you began to take responsibility for your actions blah blah . . . It's a tough world out there—you've got to learn to face it like a man "yadda yadda yadda"' routine. Anish would be slouched in Dandy's chair—Dandy *hated* when we slouched—locking eyes defiantly with him, not saying a word, the insolent smile on his face driving Dandy up the wall.

I pulled on my invisible headphones and closed my eyes, revelling in the sudden, wonderful quiet. Half an hour from now, Anish would have still not said a word, and 'Bad Cop' Dandy would storm out of his study, having lost the battle with his firstborn. This would be the cue for Mia to get started with the 'Good Cop' routine. 'Don't take what Dandy said to heart, she would say (As *if!*), he loves you very much. He is just disappointed that you are not living up to your potential blah blah.' At which point, my brother would completely lose it. He only lost it with Mia, of course, because he knew he could. And because he knew it really hurt her.

Ho hum. My life was a movie on endless replay.

I switched on the laptop. It was Anish's actually—Mia and Dandy had bought it for him last year—but it was now mine on the weekdays when he was away at school. Well, it used to be, anyway.

I checked my mail. The usual—a bunch of spam and some not-so-funny forwards from Nushki and Prerna and that jobless Raunak. I logged into FB and scrolled down the news feed. Nushki had already announced my win on her status—sweeeeet. *Yippy doo yippy yayy! Made 'Honourable Mention' at the Robotics Challenge. Congratulations, Sushma Krishna, for winning top spot—again. Bo-ring!* :P My smile paused halfway up my face. Boring? Did she really mean that? I shook my head. Naaah, of course not.

Some 32 people had 'liked' her status. That never happened with my statuses, but hey, Nushki was popular. I added my 'like' to it and scrolled down to see the comments. '*Congraaaaaaats!*' '*Superlike!*' '*When's the treat???*' '*Way to go, Nush!*' There were no '*Congrats, Sushma*' comments. Hadn't anyone read that part of the status? I shrugged. Guess that was it. People didn't read these things through. Maybe I should say something just to let people know. Not to boast or anything, but . . .

I clicked on Comment. *Thanks, Nushki! *hugs** I paused. I should say something more, especially about that *Bo-ring!* bit. People may get the wrong idea—they may think Nushki really meant it. *Not boring at all—winning is superfun.:)*

There. Now to sit back and wait.

Nushki responded almost immediately. *Okayyyy, dude—it's SUPERfun. *rolls eyes**

What did that mean? Was she being sarcastic? Just jealous that she didn't win, that's what it was.

I clicked on Chat. Forty-eight friends were online. Never mind Nushki—the other responses would start coming in any minute.

The door opened. Mia came in carrying a tray of stuff that I knew would taste uniformly awful—a big glass of skimmed-milk banana shake and a completely inadequate veggie sandwich—no butter, only a dab of margarine. I had caught her eyeing my butt with a look of complete horror last week, and since then, mealtimes had stopped being fun.

'Oh, Mia, same old garbage again?' I whined, taking off my headphones. She smiled wanly. I felt instantly ashamed. Mia never cooked—she hated it. We had always had someone come in and cook for us. But this—the stuff on the tray—she had made herself, because she wanted to be really, really sure it was low-fat and low-sugar and whatever else. 'Its OK,' I sighed exaggeratedly. 'I'll eat it.'

'Good girl,' she said. Dandy's voice rose in anger below us. Mia winced. Then she turned to me, smiling so hard it hurt me to look at her. 'So, what happened at school today?' So. She had even forgotten that today was the final of the Challenge. I felt another surge of fury against my brother, and forced myself to calm down. It didn't matter. Once I had told her my news, she would be smiling a real smile, and Anish would be forgotten.

'Well, you know, the usual,' I began. I'd keep it all nice and easy and then I'd suddenly spring it on her. She would be thrilled, particularly because Anish had also entered the Challenge in its first year. He had been so normal then. Normal by our family's standards of normal. Nerdy, geeky, super-bright. Dandy and Mia themselves had coached him for the Challenge. Anish had breezed through the first few levels. But as it got closer to the final, he began to lose interest.

He was sick of not being allowed to watch TV, he said. His brain was going to explode, he warned. He kicked a football all over the house and broke things because he wasn't allowed to go out and play with his friends (*he* always had a LOT of friends—they still hang out together on weekends). Dandy put his foot down. Mia took Dandy's side. One day, there was a huge showdown. Anish lashed out, saying that he didn't care about winning the stupid Challenge. He said Mia and Dandy were rubbish parents, they didn't care about him—all they cared about was the Challenge.

Dandy said some awful things to him then. I don't know exactly what because I had had my headphones on. In the end, Anish had dropped out of the Challenge. That's why I had signed up this year. I wanted to win it for Mia and Dandy. Strangely, they had not been so keen to coach me, which was fine—my favourite teacher at school had worked with me instead.

CRASH! Mia and I jumped at the sound, avoiding each other's eyes. It came from the study. Now it was Anish yelling. I heard my name being mentioned. '. . . and now you are ruining her too! You are making her just like yourselves, obsessed with success, disgustingly competitive! Have you even looked at her recently? Have you seen how fat she is getting, have you wondered why she has no friends . . .'

Mia turned and left the room quickly, shutting the door behind her. I pulled on the headphones, tears beginning to spill out. My brother was wrong, wrong, wrong! It wasn't my parents' fault that they didn't see me, it was his! All his! Mia and Dandy loved me to bits. And they even loved Anish—*more*. If he hadn't been such an attention-seeking loser in the first place, we could have been a happy family. Just because *he* didn't have what it took to succeed in the real world, he hated those who did.

I went back to the computer and refreshed the page. Whoaaaa! There was a whole string of comments. The first one was from the Jock. Uh oh. '*@Buttowski: It isn't winning that's boring, it's you.*' Six of my 'friends' had liked his comment. '*Lolz. Too true.*' That was one of his cronies. Then the Jock again. '*Who'd want to win against you, anyway? What if you got mad and sat on them?*' Eight likes. '*Rofl. Anyone for chapatti?*' This from a quiet mousy girl in the sixth grade who I had never spoken to in my life.

I began to shiver uncontrollably. Who were all these people I called my 'friends'? Why had I ever sent the Jock a friend request? I had been so pleased when he had accepted, feeling I was now a member of some exclusive club. Why was no one telling them to stop?

The door burst open and slammed against the wall. 'Get off my laptop—now!' yelled Anish.

It was all too much. Sobbing, I fled from the room and out of the front door. 'Sush! Sushi! Where are you going?' Mia called half-heartedly from the living room. I didn't reply. I just kept walking, not looking to the left or right. My life, as I knew it, was over. I could not go back to school. By tomorrow, the whole school would have seen Nushki's wall. I could never face all those people again, not *ever*.

I walked for two hours, in a daze, tears coursing down my face, not caring that people were giving me strange looks. What was I going to *do*? I had to have a *plan*. I glanced at my watch—I would have to head back home now or Mia and Dandy would begin to panic. I wished I was one of those daredevil teens who did cool stuff like running away from home, but I wasn't. I was just Nerd Buttowski, the girl who had no friends. I turned towards home. Not even the faintest glimmer of a plan yet, except to head back to my room, lock the door, crawl under the covers, and stay there for ever.

I slipped in through the open door and raced upstairs for the second time that day. Anish was still sitting there, at his laptop, looking at Nushki's FB wall. I felt a cold rage course through me. 'If you are done with your snooping,' I said with exaggerated politeness, 'please get out of my room.' Astoundingly, my brother got up and left, without saying a word. He didn't even chuckle.

I shut the door. Against my will, I was drawn to the computer. Might as well see all the hateful stuff. It would strengthen my resolve when I brought up the subject of changing my school with Mia and Dandy.

The screen was full of comments. I scrolled up to the *chapati* comment and began to read. The first comment after *chapati* was from Nushki, the next from—it couldn't be, surely?—Anish! Anish was Nushki's FB friend? How come *no* one told me anything?

Anoushka 'Nushki' Angelfyre
Shut up, Jock. That's not funny. That goes for the rest of you idiots as well. You know who I mean.

Anish Krishna
@Nushki: Agree. @Jock: Ever heard of cyber-bullying, dude? No? Well, I'm betting your Headmistress has.
24 likes.

Jock Menon
Hey, Anish. Was just kidding, dude. It's a joke?

Anish Krishna
Well, that's ok then. Am sure the Head will laugh too, when I tell her about it tomorrow.
33 likes.

Jock Menon
Hey man, take it easy. Will call you in ten.

Raunak Bharadwaj
Lolz. Jock's pooping his pants right now.
28 likes.

Prerna
@Anish: Go for it. I'm getting a signature campaign going. @ Jock: Game's up, saddo. You've done this to too many people for too long. @All: Want to be part of the signature campaign against bullying? 'Like' this comment.
78 likes.

I took a deep breath. A huge weight lifted off my shoulders. I exhaled slowly, deliberately, feeling the tension leave my muscles one by one.

'Sushi!' Mia and Dandy burst into my room, their faces alight with joy. My brother slouched in behind them. 'Anish tells us you won the Robotics Challenge! Congratulations!'

'Let's see the trophy!' said Dandy. I pulled it out of my backpack and handed it over. At any other time, I would have swiftly launched into the micro-details of the contest, describing how clever I'd been, and how exactly I had beaten the other competitors, but now it didn't seem that important.

'Let's celebrate!' said Mia. 'Your beloved Golden Dragon for dinner, followed by Death by Chocolate at Corner House. What say?'

'No,' I said, thinking of Anish's favourite Italian restaurant. 'Let's go to Pizzeria Napoli instead. At least I can get a salad there.' I pulled a face. 'Also, no Corner House, Mia, let's do gelato.' I paused. 'In case you've forgotten, people, I am eating healthy these days!'

My brother winked at me and grinned. 'Go for it, Buttowski!'

I stuck my tongue out at him and crossed my eyes, like I used to do when I was five. 'Ha! Won't be that for much longer, loser,' I promised.

All about Big Brothers

Anu Kumar

A journey of discovery. That was what Madhu secretly called her first visit to Mumbai, soon after she turned 12; the time she had visited her half-brother Uday who lived there with his mother. It was one of the most wonderful weeks of her life, and what had made it memorable was what she had learnt about her grandfather. All in the space of one afternoon when she had accidentally stumbled into Uday's diary.

She hadn't meant to read it actually. She had been flipping through his books, when some lines in a notebook caught her eyes, and then there was the mention of a very familiar name.

In May of 1940, Sadanand K travelled to Britain. It was the time of the Second World War, and Nazi U-boats were trawling all under the Atlantic blowing ships up, yet he reached Southampton safely and presented himself as a businessman from

New York. He was selling an exotic herbal Japanese perfume he presented to high society ladies. In a few months, as wartime privations made life hard for most Londoners, he moved to Nazi Germany.

He was still a businessman selling wonderful fragrant Japanese perfumes so no one really knew except his British superiors that he was a spy.

But Sadanand K was more than just a spy. He was a double agent, earning the confidence of his Nazi customers most of whom were high ranking bureaucrats. In a few weeks, he travelled to France, then under German occupation. His knowledge of chemicals, which made him such an expert on perfumes, earned him much appreciation from the Germans posted there. It was here in Paris and later in Nantes as he covertly assisted the secret French Resistance group that he met the love of his life, Irene.

Madhu closed the diary, opened it, shut it again, her heart beating fast. Sadanand K could be none other than her grandfather, who they both called Dadaji. Until now, Madhu realized, she had never had an idea that he was such a heroic person. He was straight out of a novel! She turned the diary over, flipped through its pages and saw filled with Uday's tiny, spidery handwriting.

She ran her fingers down the staircase of closed pages, wanting to read more but Uday would soon be back. And he would notice at once that someone had been through his notes. Uday was usually good at noticing these things.

Uday was only her half-brother. But he was the only brother she had and even though they met just twice a year, she knew what brothers were all about. In fact, Madhu could tell you all about big brothers, and she had a ready list of things she didn't quite like about Uday.

a) Big brothers are bossy

For instance, they were always ordering you about. Uday even ordered her around on mails and on Facebook. She remembered the time he had mailed to tell her that she could have his room when she visited Bombay but she had to keep it clean.

'And everyone knows boys were are far untidier!' she said indignantly to her mother, Uday's step mother.

But first Mom and then later, Dad had laughed it off.

'He's just someone who speaks his mind,' he said.

'Brothers will be brothers,' Mom had said. She quite liked Uday every time he came to visit them on Christmas.

b) Big brothers are just not bothered

She knew he had forgotten her Mom's birthday even when it was all over Facebook. And it was he who had suggested that they be nice to each other's parents. After all it wasn't their fault that his parents had separated. Uday's father had married Madhu's mother when he was just four, and so there was just a gap of five years between them. But still the way he behaved, you'd think the difference was huge.

c) Big brothers can be brusque

Last year, which was the first time she had visited him and his mother on Rakhi, he had been so brusque about it all. She had waited for him, with the decorations, the mithai and everything else but he had taken ages. Finally, it had taken him more than fifteen minutes to emerge bleary eyed from his cave. He had taken a look at the proceedings, grudgingly accepted her wishes, helped himself to a sweet, and then retreated, tossing over his shoulder, the very insulting put down, 'Oh how cute it all is.'

d) Big brothers are just not brotherly enough

His reluctant promise to give her a Rakhi gift had still not materialized. She had mentioned it to him later that same day, last year, and he had agreed, and she had a feeling he had agreed so that she would stop pestering him.

Uday also kept a record of all that she had borrowed and always did things on a *quid pro quo* basis. She hated those words, *quid pro quo*, all in big sounding Latin. For example, if you wanted Uday's fine big green and red umbrella, he would ask that she clean his bicycle for him.

He would check his books, his collection of Manga comics, his Philip Pullmans. And even after he said he was too old for Harry Potter, he gave them away only at a price. He extracted the shipping costs from her because as he said, he wasn't earning yet. And that he needed all the money he could get for his research.

'What sort of research', she had asked one late evening, as they chatted. It was just weeks after she had happened to read his diary.

And maybe it was one of those moments when Uday wasn't evasive or didn't think it beneath himself to share important things with a younger sister.

'To find out about things that Dadaji did. You didn't know, did you, that he had many fascinating adventures? And I would really love to learn all about him and find out all I can.'

It wasn't just the fact that Dadaji was mentioned in his diary. Ever since she could remember, Uday had always adored granddad. He stayed in Mumbai on his own in a small flat in Borivali. And every weekend, Uday took the train from Parel to Borivali to be with Dadaji.

Now she was curious to know what Dadaji and Uday talked about every time they met. She had thought it was all about books, especially those about travelling that they both seemed so keen about. From his Facebook updates, Madhu knew her half-brother read voraciously. He also had a blog where he put up reviews of all the books he read. But now that she had read parts of his diary, and realized his interest in Dadaji's story, she wondered if Uday was indeed thinking of writing something about Dadaji. She wished she could help him in some way.

Uday though, never gave away anything after that chat. Maybe he was embarrassed at revealing how much he looked up to Dadaji. He thought that like most girls, she would gush at how sweet he was, and Madhu for her part, wasn't going to be that predictable.

The subject of Dadaji however came up a year later, when Uday made an unusual request on Gchat.

Uday123: Can you come to Bombay this year? I hope you will. Please.

It was very unusual. Besides, he was never really so eloquent or pleading.

Mad.hu: You don't call it Mumbai?

Uday123: I know, but that's what it was called in the older days.

It was after a pause as she thought over this that she keyed in her question:

Mad.hu: Since when were you so old-fashioned?

Madhu could sound equally belligerent when she wanted.

Uday123: Oh I just like some names and stay with them. So you didn't reply? Do you think you could make it worth your while to come to Bombay? :)

She knew that the smiley that appeared could be deceptive.

Uday123: Or are you going to tell me that your mom won't allow it?

Mad.hu: I wish you'd call her Aunty or something? No, I need to come. It was your fault I didn't see Dadaji the last time.

Uday123: Oh don't remind me. Besides, Dad had overslept too, remember. Do you want me to apologize again? :(

She kept quiet. The memory of that still hurt. Uday was in Singapore with their father, when their grandfather had to be taken to hospital in Mumbai. He had had a fall, and was soon all right but they had all wanted to visit to him immediately. She was to travel with her father and Uday, because she had a weekend before school began, but because of Uday, who promised to wake their Dad up and then forgot, and they had all missed their flight. And while it hadn't mattered because her father and Uday had taken the next flight, she had school and just couldn't find more days to spare. Madhu had been miserable for days on end. She shrugged and keyed in the question she had to ask.

Mad.hu: Why now?

Uday123: I can't tell you now! It would ruin the surprise.

Mad.hu: Then you can mail me about it all later.

Her lips formed stubborn lines as she typed.

Uday123: That won't be half as convincing.

She could picture him chewing his lower lip like he always did when he was confused or thinking over things.

Mad.hu: Really? And since when have you been afflicted by a crisis of confidence?

Uday123: Listen, you must come. Please, it's for Dadaji. You would have holidays at the end of term, and then there's Rakhi.

Mad.hu: Oh, really? I would have thought you didn't really care for that festival.

Uday123: For someone who's younger by five years, you sure argue a lot.

And when he adopted that tone of voice, Madhu knew he was getting bored. But to her surprise, he didn't sign out. Instead she saw the words that appeared next, words that were quite unlike him.

Uday123: Please, Madhu, you must come.

There was a silence, and each wondered what the other was thinking about as seconds passed and then Uday's pleading words appeared again.

Uday123: It's for Dadaji. I can't explain it now, really.

Mad.hu: Ah . . .

Uday123: Don't say 'Ah . . .' like a know it all!

Mad.hu: No, but you are being so very secretive. So when you let on that little bit, it was like saying quite a lot.

Uday123: LOL! You're smart, Madhu. Believe me, it's something I'm hoping to do for him. And you must help me.

Mad.hu: OK!

She grudgingly agreed. Brothers, and their persuasive charm . . .

Uday123: Thanks! And you can have my room, remember. It has that lovely view of the sea.

Mad.hu: Big deal. You are so kind!

***

That August, it rained heavily in the way it only could in Mumbai. In hours, the roads had flooded and Uday for one looked particularly anxious.

It was very unlike him. He had lived in Mumbai for most of his life, and could tell you blasé tales of walking home for hours in rain-soaked streets, or of helping clear out flooded houses, especially those on the ground floor, when the rain water seeped in. But this year he had made elaborate plans.

They were to travel with Dadaji that wet August day. And it happened to be Rakhi as well, but Uday for his part didn't remember this.

'It is Rakhi today, you know. *So*, you *did* forget after all!'

Madhu tried not to sound indignant when she said that. He should have remembered though. After all, it was Uday who had asked her to buy a *rakhi* when she told him of her plans to be at the High Street Mall on her very first evening in Mumbai. Big brothers could be so unpredictable.

She still remembered how his voice had sounded when he had called her that evening. Urgent and pleading, like the time when they had chatted.

'Madhu, see if you can get an elegant, simple *rakhi*.'

And a little while later when she called him back, her impatience was clear. His specifications had totally confused the *rakhi* sellers.

'The two—elegant and simple—just do not go together. The *rakhi* sellers think elegant is overdone, and simple is plain. It depends on who it's for. So just tell me.'

But he had been evasive and said, 'OK, get what you really like.'

She had got two, for some reason and didn't tell him about the other one. Now she couldn't help feeling hurt that he had obviously forgotten about it all.

Still he did look excited, nervous and fidgety as they set off for Dadaji's house. It was an Uday she didn't know and she forgave him for his earlier forgetfulness.

'We're going to Panvel this time, after we pick up Dadaji from Borivali,' he told her in the train. 'I don't want Dadaji to ask too many questions. With you hopefully, he will be distracted.' He grinned impishly, his eyes crinkling up and Madhu couldn't help but smile too.

The train had filled up too soon, and she couldn't ask Uday anything else. She did wish Uday would shed a bit of light about this entire trip.

Dadaji recognized her readily when they met and that

made Madhu happier still. He smiled and his eyes vanished in the lines that covered his face. She hugged him, kneeling at his feet, with her head on his old knees.

'Come on, girl, it's only been a year or so since you last saw me. How can I forget?' His 90-year-old face still wreathed in smiles, his breath warm and comforting on her face.

'But it still is a long time, Dadaji.' Looking up at his face, she could imagine how he might have looked all those decades ago, as he travelled all over the world. She suddenly wanted to look at the old albums, to go back into the past.

'Oh, but you haven't seen as many years as I have.' Dadaji was laughing, gently tapping her cheek.

Uday was impatient to leave though he tried not to rush Dadaji too much.

'I am taking Madhu out and she wanted you to come along too. And we are going by cab so really it won't take long.' He used his gentle persuasive tone.

It was early afternoon as they set off. It would take them more than an hour to get to Panvel and cars honked impatiently around them. Big lorries grumbled by, spewing dark, heavy smoke.

'The traffic is as bad as ever,' Dadaji said, a magnificent white eyebrow raised.

Uday sitting in front with the driver, laughed, 'You mean it's worse.'

'No, it's the same. And the air is terrible. I remember the camels I rode on as we travelled along the Silk Route that time, so near the Pamirs. That part of the world saw the railways much later . . .'

As Dadaji's voice drifted into the past, Madhu noticed how still Uday had become.

'There were refugees coming from the other side,' Dadaji was speaking in a low, dreamy voice. 'People who had lost everything, dragging their feet, their heads drooping from fatigue. The Poles, the Armenians, and more, all fleeing the Russian and German armies. There was something so tragic and sad about them that we just stopped and stared. I was part of a group of merchants who traversed the Himalayas every summer. They had been doing it for centuries. And I had just joined them hoping to . . .'

Uday looked out of the window. They were on the expressway, and the wind blew his hair back. A thin sun made his pale yellow hair glint in places. He had the same kind of hair she had, genes from the same grandmother, Madhu thought.

Uday grew his hair a bit long and as the wind blew in from the window, stray tufts of it brushed across his face. She remembered how her classmates had gushed over his photos, till she had been too embarrassed to show them around anymore. She knew that embarrassment now, it was as if she didn't want to share this very different looking, very likeable brother with anyone.

'That was a terrible war, and it seemed to have taken over the world.'

Their grandfather's voice was like a gentle drone, as the car sped across the bridge. They were passing through the outer suburbs of Mumbai. Apartment buildings interspersed with mud houses, with red tiled roofs overhung by palm trees, appeared at regular intervals.

'This seems familiar.'

'Dadaji,' Uday burst in too eagerly, 'I just wanted to show Madhu the old house in Panvel.'

There was a silence. Uday had turned around, and she was struck by the pleading expression in his eyes.

'Ah, the old house,' chuckled granddad, 'Where I have been *persona non grata*, for years now . . .'

'We were just hoping to look at it,' said Uday.

'Ha, you just be careful. They might think we are claiming the property again.'

She looked at both of them, with great interest, her eyes shining. She was beginning to understand more now. So this was Uday's great secret. He had been reading up about Dadaji, and *was* indeed writing his story, the story of their grandfather, Sadanand K. A story Madhu was hoping to piece together as well.

He was a businessman, who had an expert's knowledge of every chemical that went into making wonderfully fragrant perfumes. This was how he had infiltrated the Nazi leadership. And in Paris he had fallen in love with the lovely Irene, their grandmother, who had died a decade ago, when Madhu had been three—the lady whose photo lay on granddad's table and whose books still occupied all the shelves in his room.

'I did want to see it, Dadaji,' she now said, 'The place where you spent your childhood.'

'Ah, child. I loved it too. But you see, my family would have nothing to do with me.'

'Because of Irene?' asked Uday. 'But that was a long time ago.'

'Yes, it was a long time ago, but they never accepted her. She was just a poor Irish student who came to Paris following those great writers, Joyce and Beckett and stayed on as a nurse, when the war broke out.'

'She was very lovely, wasn't she?'

'You look just like her,' he now said, turning his grey eyes towards her, and Uday grinned as she blushed.

'There's only our great-aunt in the house, now, Dadaji.' he said in turn.

'Who?'

'Great-aunt Suvarna.'

Dadaji fell quiet.

'Suvarna. My own sister who never responded to my letters. She wasn't there when I came here with Irene. And father would have nothing to do with me.'

'She did come back,' said Uday, leaning over the seat to explain. His hair falling over his forehead, his eyes blue in excitement.

'She was widowed young and was quite affected by that. She did try to make a new life for herself. And she never had your address,' Uday was speaking quickly. 'Her son knows Dad, and that's how we found him.'

They were turning into an old wicker gate now. Bushes brushed against the car, and from the gaps they could see a small, well-tended garden.

'There used to be trees there,' said Dadaji, suddenly excited. 'And a swing. And the dogs played here.'

They heard the creak of a rope being pulled and as they turned the corner, a man with a wild swinging mop of hair, half-bent with the buckets he carried on his shoulder stopped to let them pass.

'And that is Dinesh. He was the young boy father had found on the railway platform. I would know that hair anywhere.'

'Quite the Afro!' said Uday, 'Stop the car.'

Dinesh peered inside the car, his eyes wide with confusion. Dadaji spoke to him in a language that Madhu couldn't place.

But Dinesh was suddenly grinning widely. He was peering in, and exchanging news with Dadaji. If it hadn't been for their age, they would have looked like excited teenagers. Madhu could tell Suvarna was mentioned, because her name came up. It was a long while later that Dadaji turned to them, his eyes twinkling.

'She's here. And I am told she runs this place like a tyrant. Being the youngest, she always had her way.'

Then he cuffed Uday on the chin, mockingly. 'So this was your plan, wasn't it? It was deliberate. And getting this young lady here too.'

Uday looked abashed. 'I read your notes and I thought it was a pity your family didn't appreciate you enough.'

'Ah well, families can be funny. They stand behind you and then slip away too. You don't know which limits to cross but sometimes you must,' said Dadaji.

Then he turned and winked at Madhu. 'I'll tell you what. If your great aunt still tells me off, I am going to pretend to be deaf.'

He didn't have to of course. Suvarna was dumbfounded on seeing him and then for hours on end there was laughter, tears, accusations, explanations, and recriminations till they were both red with excitement.

'Father was too proud and Mom could never say anything to him. But I found her clippings about you much later. She had collected them for years, every article about you,' she told Dadaji, as Uday and Madhu listened, hardly interrupting. She had asked them to call her 'Choti Nani'.

Would, one day, Madhu wondered, she and Uday have this kind of relationship? But she knew Uday would only laugh if she aired her sentimental thoughts aloud.

'And then towards the end,' Choti Nani went on, 'Father fell sick and Ma tended to him at the cost of everything else. She died within a year of his passing.'

'Ah . . . she was always very devoted to him . . . to us too,' nodded Dadaji.

They fell silent. And then both remembered the two grandchildren who had been listening to it all.

'I forgot about the two of you. Isn't it Rakhi today? And here we are, two old people spoiling it for you.' Choti Nani spoke up again

'It is Rakhi,' Uday said, and he looked embarrassed. He looked at Madhu and she knew he had remembered after all. And she brought out the *rakhis*, the simple and elegant one she had bought as he had instructed, and the other one. He looked startled but smiled while Choti Nani blushed and then laughed, holding her head in her hands.

'It's been so long since we were together on Rakhi . . .' she said, looking at Dadaji, her eyes misting over.

'And it's the best one I could ever have wished for,' said Madhu. 'Look, you are back together after so many years.'

'Almost seven decades or more . . .' said the two of them together.

A gust of wind brought in the rain again. The maid ran out to bring in the clothes. The four of them watched a purple, heavily clouded sky, the way it looked every monsoon in Mumbai and knew even with time, some things would never change. The rains would always come to Mumbai and . . .

'Maybe I could come to Mumbai for every Rakhi!' said Madhu.

'Or wherever I happen to be,' Uday answered, though she had not expected him to. 'Or I can come to wherever you are.'

The Step Tapes

Rituparna Chatterjee

It was the last day of Rati's HAAAAW (Historic Adventures + Any Additional Adventures Week). She had coined, what she thought, was a rather intelligent acronym after much thinking. Well, she was in a 200-year-old palace after all, so historic adventures were bound to happen. True adventurers like herself must also be prepared to stumble upon any Additional Adventures, which could show up anytime and anywhere.

Unfortunately, she had been so incredibly busy avoiding Ritin that she had had no time left at all for an adventure! Or, for that matter, even for a Miss Adventure, which as Vinitha Aunty had revealed, was a special adventure in a surprising disguise which happened only to lucky little girls. Like the one last week, when they were on a chocolate-chip cookie-baking adventure. What came out of the oven looked like cookies alright, but tasted more like muffins. So they ate Muffies! Rati liked to record her adventures in her private journal and listed this under Miss Adventures.

She was annoyed with herself. All these years, Ritin had never mattered to her. Whenever she visited Vinitha Aunty, she found him perpetually buried in his tablet and an assortment of gadgets. After a while, she stopped noticing him, pretty much like she stopped noticing the painting on their living room wall. Or the more-interesting shark-like lizard which hung around on the wall on occasional summer days.

But now that Vinitha Aunty and her father had gotten married, he was suddenly her brother. '*Correction:* Stepbrother,' she told herself.

Her parents had divorced when she was just two, and after six years of rarely seeing her mum (who lived in Finland), Rati barely missed her. But she had always adored Vinitha Aunty.

Unlike the stereotypical wicked stepmother, Vinitha Aunty was the best mom she could have asked for. Their neighbour for all these years, Vinitha Aunty pampered her and even looked after her when Papa was away on business trips. She felt close to Vinitha Aunty, who worked as a marketing executive in a toy company. She was smart, intelligent, loving and super fun. Rati knew what she wanted to be when she grew up. She wanted to be Vinitha Aunty! Except for one crucial difference: she didn't want to work in a toy company but do something more grown-up and adventurous. She wanted to be an archaeologist.

When her dad had hesitatingly asked her if she approved of the 'suggestion' of having a new mommy in the form of

Vinitha Aunty, she had hugged him and said 'Yes, yes, I do!'. Now, she could have both Papa and Vinitha Aunty.

But Ritin had suddenly appeared from nowhere and become a major obstacle. Her little time with Papa was now cut in half. For example, the week before, Papa had cancelled their super-sacred Sunday brunch ritual at Big Chill, to go watch the vintage car rally with Ritin. Papa had invited her, and when she declined, promised to get her a piece of her favourite Squidgy Chocolate Cake. Although, she was dying to see those gleaming historic automobiles, she'd rather study than go with Ritin, never mind the Squidgy Chocolate Cake.

Meanwhile, Vinitha Aunty, the darling that she was, had stayed back. They had all kinds of girly adventures like making Play-Doh creatures except that you could eat these because they were made out of yummy marzipan. And then there were Muffies. She loved it! But she missed her dad. Why couldn't she be with both of them. Why couldn't they just send this cold Ritin to boarding school and let her stay behind?

Until now, she was convinced that Ritin was not human. She thought he was some kind of a machine sent by aliens to study human behaviour. He was glued to gadgets because he was constantly transmitting signals through them. She had tried to warn her dad, who laughed it away. Even if Papa did not believe her, she had to be on alert. Rati had even nervously told Vinitha Aunty, afraid that she might be angry at her son being called an alien conspiracy. But Vinitha Aunty being the rock-star that she was simply winked and whispered, 'I know honey!'

They were at her granny's house. '*Correction: haveli,*' she chided herself. Papa and Vinitha Aunty were both away on business trips. How she had begged them to take her with them. She'd stay quietly in the hotel room and watch TV all day long and paint and be a good girl. They wouldn't even notice that she was there.

Instead, she had been left behind with her least favourite person in her most favourite place.

'You guys need to get to know each other. After all, you're siblings now,' said Papa.

'Um . . . step siblings,' Rati corrected her father.

'Come on now Rati. You finally have a real brother to smear with tilak on Bhai Dooj, rather than Chhotu,' said Papa.

'You can never compare a boy to a dog. Especially a step-statue brother to Chhotu,' said Rati stomping off.

The *haveli*, called Raahat Bhavan, was located just outside of Jaipur. Made in 1760, it was designed specifically to give its residents *raahat* (meaning relief) from the fiery desert heat. The strategic positioning of its windows utilized natural winds thereby creating an illusion of mysterious invisible fans at work. Raahat Bhavan's thick stone walls, high ceilings, and its endless dark cool corridors provided magically natural cool comfort.

Rati's holidays in Raahat Mahal had been few and far between. But they were memorable, full of fun and fantasy, as all holidays in *havelis* have a way of being. Occasionally, local women came to the *haveli* and Daadi used to teach them things like language and arithmetic. Rati would watch them for hours fascinated by the myriad bright hues of their *ghagra-kabjas*, and their bold *kohl*-lined eyes.

At the *haveli*, alone together, Ritin had even tried to

be nice to Rati, inviting her to play on his PSP with him. He was like a tortoise carrying his world on his back, in his backpack. And like she had guessed, it was full of all sorts of useless game-related gizmos. He was always digging in it, sort of like how Chhotu and she 'excavated' their neighbourhood park for 14th-century treasures.

'No thanks, I prefer Wii,' she said politely and walked off.

Was there a clue of him being an actual human, now that he was being warm?

'*Trying* to be warm,' said Rati in her characteristic style. An adventurer, especially an upcoming archaeologist, must never let her guard down, especially around suspicious creatures.

As usual it was time for Daadi's afternoon siesta. Her snores echoed through the *haveli's* dark, cool corridors. Frustrated with her zero adventures, or even Miss Adventures, and unable to sleep, Rati took a walk through one of the corridors. She had her camera strapped on her neck, for emergency recordings, which she could then put into her diary. A blinding light waited patiently at the end, and as if hypnotized, Rati walked towards it.

At the edge, was a spider, spinning a complex web. At night, the tube lights would be turned on, attracting a variety of insects, some of which could get trapped here, while lizards would take care of the others. Rati thought it was fascinating and continued to watch the spider in rapture.

'Hey, come here. Look what I found. Far more interesting spinning here, than your boring spider.' What? Could it be that Ritin had abandoned his gadgets for once? Had he really turned human? Anyway, she must not go, in case it was an alien plot to capture her. But it was so tempting!

Giving in and burning with curiosity, she tiptoed towards him cautiously.

'Closer, look here,' he said. He was kneeling down holding a small plastic rectangle in his hand. Was it really what she thought it was?

'Yes, it really is a cassette!' said Ritin.

The history buff in Rati was ecstatic! She had heard of cassettes but she had never seen one in real life. How could she? Cassettes were almost obsolete. 'Where did you find this?' Rati asked urgently.

'Right up there . . . there's a whole stack of them,' he said, pointing to a shelf on the whitewashed stone wall, right by the intricately-carved ventilator and beside a lamp.

'I've seen these before. See, everything is on this reel of magnetic tape. The player spins it and it plays.' Rati was furious at herself—she had been here before, and this cold-alien-conspiracy-statue had seen it on his very first trip.

'That's one of the perks of being older,' Ritin said, reading her thoughts.

Rati, suspicious as ever, asked, 'But how can you be so sure about how it works?'

'Ramesh Uncle explained it to me.'

Papa explained it to him. To h-i-m! And not her? Rati was fuming.

'He says I'm too digital and must at least understand a few mechanical and analog concepts. Ramesh Uncle will soon be teaching me how to solder and eventually take me to lathe classes as well. I can't wait to use my hands on some real machines.'

'Wait, you call him Uncle too?' asked Rati, somewhat relieved that he was still only her Papa.

'Yes, well, just like you still call Ma, Vinitha Aunty. You're not used to it yet either, are you?' Rati was embarrassed. Ritin was suddenly getting less creepy by the second, which was a pretty creepy thing on its own!

'Well, ummm . . . actually, I don't know how to tell you this. But I think I should,' Ritin said after a long pause. 'You see, you're rather fond of my Ma. But you're younger, it's easier for you. You practically have no memory of your own mother, right? But I remember my Dad, and I miss him. But I also hate the way he treated Ma. She's so happy now,' he said softly. 'It's very hard to wake up one fine day and call someone else Dad. And worse, there's a stepsister attached in the package. I'm sorry I was so cold to you . . . practically like a cold alien statue.'

Rati cringed. She hated the 'step' prefix attached to her. She realized how alike they were. She didn't know where to look. How could he have read her exact thoughts?

'At first I hated you. There you were with ribbons in your hair always jumping and ready for an adventure. But you're not so bad,' he smiled. 'You see, like you, I too am adjusting. But I must admit, your dad's a great guy.'

'So is Vinitha Aunty. She understands that I'm a girl and not all girls are interested in lathe machines.'

'Haha! Yes, you're right,' Ritin said with a smile. 'Now, let's go hide the tape before Daadi wakes up. You do know, we aren't supposed to be going through all this. These must be private recordings,' he said, holding out the cassette and its box for Rati to see.

Rati was quivering with excitement at this treasure. She ran her fingers over the cracked plastic cover. Nestling inside was a worn out yellowing paper with faded handwriting.

She assumed this was Urdu. What was inside it? Perhaps, confidential cryptic voice messages were inside. A dozen questions swarmed through Rati's head leaving her slightly giddy with curiosity and excitement.

'Let's explore the rest of the boxes and stash it away before anybody comes,' said Ritin.

Rati was now holding a cassette in her hands. A real cassette. A real, vintage treasure! This was so much better than undertaking excavations in the neighbourhood garden. And she had a real partner, who was not her dog.

'See, you can totally pull the tape out and then put it back in and I believe it will still work,' said Ritin. He rolled his finger through the groovy hole in the cassette and using his other hand, he pulled out a few inches of the magnetic tape out of its plastic holder. Then he simply reversed his motions and put it all back in together. Rati watched fascinated.

'Let me try it,' she said pulling out some tape and carefully rolling it all back together.

'Isn't this spinning fun?' Rati grinned and nodded. It was indeed! Rati now understood that the music word 'rewind' actually meant physically winding the tape up. So cool! They took turns, each time unrolling more and more of the smooth ribbon and putting it back.

'Oh, I know! Let's have a spinning contest,' Rati suddenly suggested.

'Ssh, lower your voice, remember we're trespassing on private property. And trespassers are always prosecuted,' said Ritin.

'OK, OK!' Rati lowered her voice down to an urgent stream of whispers. 'So, whoever pulls out the most and puts it back the fastest, wins. I'm smaller, so I go first,' said Rati. Before Ritin could respond, she pulled and pulled and jerked off a long ribbon of tape. Rati ran through the corridor. Her endless ribbon tail merged with the darkness.

And then the faintest flick danced across the walls and echoed through the corridor's empty hollowness. Rati looked and to her horror realized that she had snapped the tape. She was really scared. It wasn't just a cassette. It was a piece of history, worse, a private piece of history. It was somebody's precious belonging and she had damaged it. Large salty drops of fear rolled off her big cheeks, somewhat soaking her T-shirt.

'We'll fix it, we'll fix it. Don't worry,' said Ritin, running towards her. 'But we must hurry. It's a long mess and there is no time to cry. Be the big eight-year-old that you are now.'

'Eight, going on nine,' corrected Rati angrily, wiping the tears away.

'All the more reason then,' said Ritin.

He had now started to rewind the roll of tape. Rati helped by holding up the closest bunch of the excess tape on the floor, keeping it ready for rolling. They did this as meticulously and quickly as anyone possibly could. Unfortunately, the tape had knotted up. They continued to wrap it up the best as they could, knots and all. Eventually, Ritin had a small spool of tape in his hands. Just a couple of feet more and they'd be done. They could then start rewinding it in the cassette.

Just then, they felt a tug. It seemed bigger than the small knots, most of which they had painstakingly removed, and it seemed to come from above. They looked up and noticed that some of the ribbon was stuck behind the lamp on the wall, right next to the shelf where they had originally found the cassettes.

The cool evening breeze must have lifted the almost weightless tape causing it to get stuck there. Ritin, being the taller one, hopped and pulled gently, but with no luck.

Rati, who knew the *haveli* well from previous holidays ran to the store room and got out a black umbrella with a sharp metal tip. This relic was one of her very own discoveries, from former exploratory missions.

'Great thinking,' said Ritin. He shoved the umbrella's tip, trying to fish out the tape, which had wrapped around the lamp. They tried several times. But neither the gaming aficionado nor the upcoming archaeologist had kite-flying or fishing skills, which could have been handy in this situation.

Ritin was rather frustrated. His hand ached to the point of cramping. Why should he even put up with this. It wasn't his fault after all. Whether step, real or cousin, sisters were always trouble, he thought as he impatiently shoved the umbrella from his right to his raised left hand.

SMASH!

'What happened, who is that!' screamed Daadi, suddenly awakened by the crashing noise that travelled through the whole *haveli*. While exchanging the umbrella from one hand to another, Ritin had mistakenly shattered the beautiful vintage lamp. The trapped tape fell on the floor along with the glass in smithereens.

'Quick, shove it all in your backpack,' said Rati, pulling Ritin's backpack and already starting to do as she said.

'How would that help?' said Ritin.

He was scared. He knew he was in trouble because this was not just another lamp but an expensive antique, as most things in the *haveli* were. The kids had been told to be as careful around the *haveli*, as they would have been in a museum. And although Rati had created the tape mess, Ritin had broken an antique treasure.

'What is it?' asked Daadi. Echoes of the *thak-thak* of her *lathi* got louder and louder, which meant she was close. By now Rati had packed the empty cassette, its cover, and the knotted spool of tape in Ritin's backpack.

'I know Daadi! There that one did it,' Rati quipped pointing right at Ritin's head. He looked baffled by her betrayal, that too, after all this . . . after all the trouble he had taken for her.

'Argh, I knew it! The pests!' said Daadi, looking angrily right behind Ritin. He looked up and saw two pigeons behind, clucking away. He let out a sigh of relief. 'This is not the first time they have smashed something here. If only I knew how to get rid of them. But they have been here much longer than I have,' said Daadi.

Ritin was ashamed. Rati had stood up for him and he had doubted her. 'Anyway, Ramesh will be here any minute and can help fix this mess. I keep telling him, donate these antiques to the museum. Just no point keeping them,' said Daadi.

'Here we are!' Rati heard her Papa's voice as he emerged from the shadows with Vinitha Aunty. 'Did you kids trouble Daadi much? Rati did you fight with Ritin?' asked Papa, bending down and holding his hands out for Rati.

'No, no Rati is a darling. Ritin, I hope you at least got your head out of your games for a little while, and kept her company,' said Vinitha Aunty, hugging Ritin.

'Come, come, tomorrow is Bhai Dooj. Our first as a

family!' said Daadi as they walked towards the living room.

'Rati, you won't believe the gift I've got for you to give Ritin tomorrow,' said Vinitha Aunty. 'But only if you want to of course,' she said hesitatingly.

'Why won't she? Ritin is a fine boy and will be giving her a present which she will absolutely love. But ssshh! It's a surprise until tomorrow morning,' said Papa.

Ritin and Rati smiled at each other. Oblivious to what had happened, the elders smiled, relieved that they finally seemed to like each other, and kept walking, heading to their rooms.

'You know kids, no more cold wars. Bhai Dooj is all about sharing. You should be grateful that you have each other,' said Daadi.

Rati and Ritin had shared much more. They had shared a secret adventure, which some might believe was a Miss Adventure. And now, like lakhs of siblings, they too waited for the big Bhai Dooj morning, and, of course, the presents they would give each other. But they were far more excited about their next big adventure together, and for that they simply couldn't wait.

As they lay in their beds that night in Daadi's room, they went over their big day.

'Maybe, we'll find a cassette player next time,' said Rati.

'Or perhaps, I can learn to build one.'

'Yes! And then, we can finally know what was in those tapes,' said Rati, falling asleep.

The Henna Boys

Deepa Agarwal

Ma finished braiding Rani's curly black hair and threaded a red ribbon into it. Jagga watched, his thin face sullen. His eyes softened when his six-year-old sister began to slip shimmering glass bangles on her little wrists. Suddenly, someone knocked. Roop, their older brother, almost grown-up at sixteen, hurried to open the door.

'Is she ready?' Sunita Maasi, Ma's sister, bustled in. Stout, resplendent in a turmeric-yellow sari, her gold bracelets jangled as she bent to kiss Rani. 'Come on,' she said. 'It's already nine o'clock. Your uncle has to leave for work.' The remaining bangles slid out of Rani's hand as Sunita Maasi pulled her away.

Ma hugged Rani and Jagga, who had just turned twelve, picked up the shabby cloth bag that held her clothes. Silently, he and Roop followed their aunt out of the shanty, a crude structure of old bricks roofed with plastic sheets. Her husband waited in the rutted lane, leaning against his scooter. Within minutes, they sped off, carrying Rani away.

'Why did you let her go?' Jagga burst out, the moment they re-entered the shack, already stuffy in the April heat.

Roop's long, bony face became uneasy. 'Jagga!' He put a hand on his brother's arm. 'Show some respect.'

'Respect!' Jagga cried. 'Baba never bothered about us. And now Ma's letting Sunita Maasi take Rani away. As if we can't take care of her!'

'It's just for a day or two . . .' Ma's tired face grew pinched. 'Sunita and her husband plan to visit the shrine of Vaishno Devi to seek the goddess's blessings. When will Rani ever get a chance like that?'

Jagga's eye fell on the small glass bangles, lying abandoned on the mud floor. He'd bought them yesterday. That's all they could manage, he thought bitterly, a few glass bangles, resisting the urge to fling them outside. 'You're right,' he said, turning away abruptly. 'We'll never be able to do anything like that for Rani.'

'Jagga . . .' Ma's thin hand felt heavy on his shoulder. 'She'll be back soon, son. Have your breakfast.'

Jagga wanted to yell out, 'I'm not hungry!' But Ma's tearful voice stopped him.

Reluctantly he sat down cross-legged on the floor next to Roop, and gulped down cold *chapattis* leftover from last night with mouthfuls of hot, sweet tea.

Then Roop picked up the bag that contained the tools of their trade—plastic cones filled with henna paste, and the boys headed for the bus stop.

It was almost eleven when they reached the Hanuman

temple. Some of the other henna artists were already busy, tracing patterns on women's palms. But the brothers' place was at the end of the row, far from the temple. This meant that they got customers only after all the others were occupied. Of course, it was different at festivals and during the wedding season. Since it was considered auspicious, almost a must, for women to decorate their hands with henna on such occasions, there was plenty of work then.

The sun was climbing higher above the tall buildings on the other side of the road. It was unbearably hot now.

'Who'd come out in this weather?' Jagga grumbled, pushing his straggly hair off his broad forehead and fanning himself with a piece of cardboard.

'Patience!' Roop said. 'See, the queue's nearly reached the big tree.'

Jagga shrugged his skinny shoulders, almost lost in his faded, outsized shirt. The stream of worshippers heading for the temple *was* growing. It was Tuesday, a day sacred to the monkey god, and this was one of the most popular temples in Delhi. The sweet sellers were doing brisk business, as were flower sellers. Suddenly Roop said, 'Why did you shout like that? You know Ma tries to do her best.'

Jagga frowned.

'I know that . . .' he said, 'and . . . it's nice for Rani . . . that Sunita Maasi gives her those treats we can't afford. But I'm scared, Roop . . . scared that one day Rani might not want to come back. You know how desperate Sunita Maasi is to adopt her.' His voice choked up.

'Ma hasn't agreed so far has she?' Roop said.

'That's because we make such a fuss! And Rani refuses to leave us too!"

Roop sighed.

'Maybe . . . it might be best for her.'

Jagga gaped, horrified. True, Sunita Maasi was much better off. Her husband worked as a driver with the government and earned a decent salary. They lived in a flat with electricity and running water. But they had no children and Sunita Maasi felt the lack keenly. That's why she kept pestering Ma to let her adopt Rani. Perhaps she felt Ma would part more readily with a daughter than one of her sons. Ma might have given in if both the boys hadn't always protested so strongly.

And now Roop, too, was saying it might be best for Rani. Jagga felt tears sting his eyelids. 'How can it be best for her?' he wanted to shout. 'To leave her own mother and brothers and live with Sunita Maasi, even if she's richer?'

Roop continued softly, as if he'd read Jagga's mind. 'Jagga, I can't bear to part with Rani either. But the more I think about it, I feel we're being selfish. Sunita Maasi can give her so much that we can't.'

'I can't think like that,' Jagga replied abruptly. This exchange had made his head ache so hard that it became unbearable. To distract himself, he picked up one of the henna cones. He began to squeeze out the green henna paste from its tip, drawing a peacock, something he had recently learned, on his own palm.

'Stop wasting!' Roop's face turned irritable.

Jagga stopped with a guilty start.

Then he noticed two women heading towards them. A curly-haired girl, dressed in a pair of jeans and a T-shirt, who was skipping ahead of the two women, suddenly halted. She seemed the same age as Rani. She giggled, making Jagga blush. He could guess what she must be thinking. A boy decorating his own hand with henna—how silly! His friends had made fun of him too. But they shut up when he told them bluntly that his father was in prison again and he had to earn something, somehow. Besides, Roop had already begun to sit in the small bazaar near the temple. Women came to shop for glass bangles and other trinkets there after their prayers. Sometimes they stopped to have their palms decorated with henna.

Their mother too had said that it was not a trade for a boy. But when Roop, who learnt the art from a friend, began to bring in money, she had to accept it. They could not depend on his father's earnings, and what she made, cleaning houses, was not enough to live on. By the time Jagga joined Roop, she didn't react at all.

'Not bad,' he heard the taller lady say.

'Madam, we can draw all these patterns.' Roop flipped open the album that had cost so much to prepare. The women leafed through it curiously.

'Can he make a little Appu on my hand? Like this?' The girl held out the stuffed cloth elephant she was carrying. Decorated with bright embroidery and small round mirrors, it had a battered looking trunk.

'Oh, you and your Appu!' said her mother. 'That's not a regular henna pattern.'

'But it can be!' Jagga exclaimed, seeing the girl's face drop. 'Come, I'll make an Appu on your hand.'

Roop threw him a disbelieving look. Jagga smiled and a little shakily, began to work on the elephant. And soon, *everyone* was smiling!

'I want an elephant on my hand too,' someone cried. It was a small boy. Jagga got busy again.

After that, to their delight, customers poured in, all of them children accompanying their parents. Jagga drew more henna elephants on tiny palms, bears, even a rather convincing monkey. And when the brothers boarded the bus that would carry them back to their hut in the shantytown, Jagga's arms were aching.

But he was walking on air. They had earned almost five hundred rupees. How happy Ma would be!

'That was a really smart thing you did, Jagga!' Roop slapped his back. 'Tomorrow, a new shirt for you. And a proper hair-cut. If we look neat and smart, people might ask us to come to their homes to decorate women's hands at weddings. That's where the real money is! And if we can prove we're really good, we could even make up to 7000 rupees in a day—they say you can charge 5000 rupees for the bride—a hundred each for the other women. Imagine!'

Jagga grinned. His quiet brother was in unusually high spirits today. 'Hanumanji willing, maybe we will one day soon. And . . . we'll buy a pair of jeans for Rani too,' he said. 'The kind that girl was wearing.'

'Jagga!' Roop laughed. 'They were rich people.'

'So what?' Jagga replied. 'If we earn enough our Rani can be as well-dressed as anyone! Oh, let's buy some *gulab jamuns*!' he cried, as his eye fell on the round sweets, fat with syrup, in a nearby shop. 'Rani loves them . . .' He stopped abruptly, remembering that Rani wasn't at home.

'We all love them,' Roop said quickly. 'Let's take six.'

Jagga sighed. But despite his gloom, as they rode home on the bus, he couldn't help dreaming. What if they could make this much money every day? They might even be able to forget that their father was in jail for the next five years for picking pockets. Rani could go to school, it didn't matter that both her brothers had to drop out. And suddenly Sunita Maasi didn't seem that much of a threat . . .

It was almost nine when they reached home. Traffic was always heavy in the city and they had to walk some distance through the narrow lanes to reach their shack.

The moment they entered, Jagga's face darkened again. The room felt so empty. Even his mother's cry of delight, 'What, so much money!' failed to cheer him. He swallowed his dinner silently, even though Ma had cooked his favourite *aloo* curry, fiery with chillies.

Then he pulled out his straw mat and spread it outside the hut. It was cooler there, in the open. After a while his brother joined him. Jagga covered himself with his worn cotton sheet, turned his back on Roop and tried to sleep. But his restless thoughts wouldn't let him. Was it really better for Rani to leave her own family so she could lead a more comfortable life?

The breeze blowing gently against his hot cheeks suddenly turned harsh. It gathered up dust from the road, dried leaves and bits of paper, and flung them about. Then it tried to pull Jagga's sheet away. He sat up hurriedly, clinging to it.

The wind was howling now and Jagga groaned as the street lights beyond the *basti* blew out abruptly. Lightning crackled, then forked menacingly across the black sky, making his heart thump. The metal sheets roofing the other shanties set up a deafening rattle, a can fell over with a crash, and a baby began to wail.

'It's a dust storm!' Roop screamed, bundling up his sheet. 'Get inside.'

Jagga was rolling up his mat when he noticed that the black plastic sheets that roofed their hut were flapping wildly. He gasped as one of the large stones that held them in place rolled off.

'Roop! Our roof!' He flung down the mat and caught hold of the sheet. But the wind was going crazy. It tore the flimsy plastic out of his hands. Quickly Roop grabbed the other end. Both boys struggled to keep the sheets in place. Ma hurried out to help too. But one by one all the stones rolled away, and suddenly they were left with their roof in their hands . . .

'Praise Hanumanji, it didn't rain!' Ma said, pouring tea into their glasses. The boys were in no mood to talk. A pale light was spreading over the *basti* and they could see destruction all around. 'I'm glad Rani wasn't here.'

Jagga put down his glass. His throat choked up so hard that he couldn't swallow. Yes . . . Rani was terrified of storms. Roop's dark face looked pinched as he stared into his tea.

'Finish your breakfast,' Ma said, passing them more cold chapattis. 'We have to put the roof back.'

What else could they do? Jagga swallowed the dry chapatti and sprang to his feet.

'Come on, Roop,' he said. 'We're lucky we could save the plastic sheets.'

Roop nodded. They gathered up all the stones they could find, then began to stretch the sheets over the walls, draping the plastic over the roof beam. Ma held on from one side, Roop from the other, while Jagga climbed up to put the stones back.

'Here, here's another.' Salma, their next door neighbor, held up a stone. Jagga smiled and thanked her.

'So you managed to save your sheets too? Not everyone was as lucky. What a night!' Anand exclaimed from across the lane. Like them he was up on his roof, his young daughters helping him replace it.

'Glad to see you're still here, Roop,' Anand's wife Lakshmi called out as she swept up the rubbish. 'I was afraid the storm might have blown you away!'

'Too bad, auntie,' Roop grinned. 'I would have had a free ride to some exotic place.'

There was a burst of laughter from all the people busy repairing their damaged homes, and Jagga felt his heart lighten.

'We badly need to get metal sheets for the roof,' Roop said, as they waited for their bus.

'Yes,' Jagga sighed. 'If we have another good day . . .'

And then, someone called out, 'Roop! Jagga!'

It was Sunita Maasi, seated in a rickshaw with a small curly-haired girl!

'Rani!' Jagga yelled. 'What are you doing here?'

Rani jumped off the rickshaw and ran to him.

'This girl!' Sunita Maasi fumed. 'She's impossible!'

'Why?' Jagga frowned.

'She cried all night. She said she was scared of the storm and wanted to go home.'

'But Rani, you were much safer in Sunita Maasi's flat!' Jagga cried. 'Do you know . . .' he hesitated, then went on, 'our roof blew off?'

In reply Rani just clung to him.

'Weren't you leaving for Vaishno Devi today?' Roop asked.

'We couldn't because of this silly girl!' Sunita Maasi replied.

'Rani, you've missed a wonderful chance,' Jagga said.

'I want to be with Ma! And Roop Bhaiya and you!' Rani pouted.

'Oh, you silly, silly girl!' Jagga hugged her. 'Come, I think there are some *gulab jamuns* for you! And you know what? I'm going to draw a henna elephant on your hand!'

And many, many more elephants, bears and peacocks, he thought happily!

A Witch's Gift

Ani Sengupta

I

In the remote village of Basera, somewhere in the hills of Uttar Pradesh lived a girl called Maya, who sang hymns of Lord Krishna every morning at the temple. She would wake up at five, take a bath and then string a garland of marigold flowers and leaves before making her way to the temple. Praying for her brother's prosperity and wellbeing in the hopes that he would soon be able to afford visiting her more than once a year. While she was in sixth grade at the local school, her brother had been sent off to attend Junior College in the city.

After their parents died five years ago, their aunt and uncle who had no children adopted them and treated them as their own. Her uncle would say that Maya was a replica of her mother with her doe-like eyes on a wheatish and somewhat round face, a contagious bright smile and her ever-helping nature that earned her everyone's affection.

However, he did not approve of her helping one particular old woman who lived at the end of the village across the woods. Rumour had it that this woman practiced witchcraft but Maya laughed at the claims. She was determined to help the old woman who saved her brother's life from a deadly snakebite a few years ago.

'If you don't let me go, she might curse you,' she would smirk at her uncle's warnings.

A little annoyed and a little fearful, he would grumble but let her go as long as she promised to be home before sunset. That evening too, like every other evening, Maya made her way through the paddy fields to reach the old woman's hut. She swept the floors, cleaned the utensils and began tidying the room. But her mind was on Rakshabandhan, and she was sad that she didn't have money to send a *rakhi* to her brother. She couldn't get herself to ask her Uncle; after all the trouble he went through to pay for their education.

'Why do you look sad today?' asked the old woman laying in bed.

'Oh no, I'm just preoccupied,' replied Maya.

'I have something special for you,' said the old woman huddled up in bed and pointing to a wooden box in the corner.

'What is it, Daadi?'

'Take what you want from it,' she said smiling, showing her bare gums.

She looked frail with sunken eyes and cheeks and receding, white, unkempt hair. As she sat up on the bed, adjusting her thick glasses with her crooked, wrinkled fingers, Maya cautiously opened the box, her hands trembling as she looked inside.

'Daa-dii . . . where did you get these?' she asked, her voice quivering. 'You mustn't keep them out like this.'

'Humph . . . do you think thieves will dare enter a witch's hut?' she laughed.

'They are beautiful,' said Maya, pulling out a shiny golden necklace with glittering green and white stones all over.

'You can have it if you want.'

'No . . . no. I don't need it.'

'Look under the jewellery. I have a special *rakhi* for you there.'

'How did you know I was thinking . . .'

'Is it this one?' she asked holding a gold and silver coloured lotus made from silk and coloured mesh with a bright, red stone shining in the centre. The bands were red ribbons with silver embroidery on the sides.

'This is so beautiful Daadi.'

The old woman nodded. 'It is a special *rakhi*,' she said. 'Just for you.'

'But how will I send it? I have no money to post it.'

'Give it to Khan Chacha. He'll take it to the city with him tomorrow.'

'But are you sure I can have this? It looks very expensive.'

The woman laughed and nodded again.

'Thank you, Daadi,' said Maya and hugged her.

'Now hurry before you miss Khan Chacha at the electricals shop.'

Maya thanked her again and ran as quickly as she

could, cutting through the woods and across paddy fields, the *rakhi* dangling from her hand. Khan Chacha was her only hope.

'There . . . it will be safe here,' he assured her, putting the *rakhi* in his pocket and stroking his henna-coloured beard.

'I'll give it to your brother as soon as I reach,' he said, smiling on seeing her excitement.

II

The next morning, Khan Chacha set out for the city by bus, stopping by his sister's village for lunch. The ride was a bumpy one and heavy rains had eaten into the tar road, which was now fraught with potholes. Four hours of tiresome journeying and Khan Chacha was ready to jump off the bus. As they pulled up to his sister's village, the conductor asked to check his ticket. A little annoyed but eager to get down, he pulled it out of his pocket and mumbled something about the ticket checker to the driver as he left.

'*Naya hai*,' said the driver laughing and wished Khan Chacha a good day.

He was thrilled to see his sister and nieces who ran to him and hugged him. While he washed his hands and feet, his nieces were busy rummaging through his bag and pockets for gifts.

'Be careful now,' he said. 'I have a *rakhi* in my pocket for someone.'

But the girls kept at it and eventually found their gifts in his bag, two plastic dolls with colourful dresses, wrapped in brown paper. He laughed happily seeing their excitement.

After a hearty lunch of spicy and succulent mutton and rotis, it was time for him to take the next bus to the city. His nieces would not let him go and after much promising and assuring that he would stop by on his way back, and a stern look from their mother, the two girls led him to the door.

As he bid them goodbye, he put his hand over his pocket searching for the *rakhi*. Suddenly, his smile disappeared.

'What is it, Bhaiyya?' asked his sister, a little perturbed.

'The *rakhi*. It isn't in my pocket . . .'

'Did you two find a *rakhi* in Mamaji's pocket?' his sister asked the two girls.

They shook their heads innocently.

III

It had fallen on his seat in the bus when he pulled out his ticket for the conductor.

But not for long. A little girl who boarded the bus with her mother at the very next stop, discovered it. She was dazzled by the shiny red stone, which matched the colour of her dress.

'Ma, look what I found,' she said, holding out the *rakhi*.

'Tsk, someone must have forgotten it here. Give it to the conductor and he'll return it.'

'No. It is mine now.'

'But we already bought *rakhis* for your cousins.'

'No, this is mine.'

'Conductor!' called out the girl's mother.

'Was there a girl sitting on this seat before us? She forgot her *rakhi* on the seat.'

'No girl. There was an old man. Why don't you keep it?' he said, seeing the little girl stick out her lower lip.

'All right, I guess you can keep it,' said her mother handing the *rakhi* back to her.

Before her mother could change her mind, the girl quickly tied it to her left hand and held it near the window, watching the red stone sparkle in the sunlight. But soon after, she felt the *rakhi*'s grip tighten on her wrist. Uncomfortable, she pulled at it, trying to loosen it, but the more she pulled, the tighter it got. Helpless and annoyed, she began crying, holding out her arm to her mother who untied the knot for her. Just then the bus braked sharply and the *rakhi* flew out of the window, landing on the dusty road, and the bus moved on.

It lay there shining in the sunlight, dodging buses and bullock carts and occasional bicycles and cars as they rode past, some getting close but none driving over it.

IV

'Hey Ravi, look!' said a boy, pointing to a *rakhi* lying in the middle of the road.

'Be careful Golu,' warned his older brother but Golu ran to fetch it.

Their driver had pulled up to the side of the road after the car engine heated up. They were on their way back home from the hills, just in time for Rakshabandhan, the next morning. It was the elaborate meal prepared by their aunt that excited the two boys more than the Rakhi ceremony.

'Golu, come back here,' shouted his father from the car. 'How many times do I have to tell you not to cross a road alone.'

'And stop picking rubbish from the roads,' reprimanded his mother.

'It's nice, *haan*?' said Golu, dismissing his parents remarks.

'It's a *rakhi* silly,' said his brother. 'You're not a girl. Throw it.'

'No, I'll give it to Mansi Didi.'

'So you can tie it to her arm?' laughed Ravi. 'She already has two for us. And if I tell her that you found it on the road, she'll throw it anyway.'

Golu shrugged and put it in his pocket before his brother snatched it away.

The driver returned shortly with two tumblers filled with water, poured them into the radiator and then turned on the engine. It revved into life and they were on their way again.

Golu placed the *rakhi* on his hand, watching the red stone glitter, its two ends fluttering with the wind. He tried tying them to his wrist, but they slipped. He tried again but they kept slipping as the car bounced from pothole to pothole. A few tries later, he gave up and let it fall to the floor. By the time they reached home, he had forgotten all about it.

'*Chote sahib*, do you want this *rakhi*?' asked the driver, after cleaning the car.

Golu shook his head.

'I'll take it for my daughter then,' he said and put it in his pocket.

V

The next day was Rakshabandhan and the driver's ten-year-old daughter Mini was up early, preparing for the occasion. She washed a silver-coloured plate, where she placed her hand-made *rakhis*, some rice granules, *roli*, *agarbatti*, sweets and a *diya*. Then she wore her favourite blue skirt from her last birthday and waited for her neighbour and his friend to arrive. Her hair was neatly braided with two purple clips on either side and she wore lots of plastic bangles of different colours on both hands.

'Papa, look I made these,' she said showing him two blue and yellow flower *rakhis* made from sponge and shiny paper stuck over a braided band.

'They're nice,' he said, patting her head. 'I forgot to tell you that I found one in the car yesterday. Look in my pant pockets, will you?'

'This is beautiful,' said Mini, holding it on her palm. 'It's better than the ones I made.'

'But you made these. That's more important.'

Just then the bell rang, and Mini ran to open the door. Her neighbour, who was her *rakhi* brother, knew that she would be fasting until she tied him a *rakhi*, so he made it a point to get to her house as early as possible. Besides, he loved the *puri* and *chole* that her mother would have prepared for him, not to mention the *gulab jamuns* after.

He was short and stubby while his friend had a tall and lean physique, with glasses on a thick nose and beady deep-set eyes, giving him a studious and somewhat serious demeanour. Mini thought they looked like characters from a cartoon series.

The ceremony began with Mini holding the plate near her neighbour's face, and making three clockwise circles around it, then applying *roli* on his forehead and sprinkling some rice granules on his head. As her mother helped hold the plate, she tied one of the *rakhis* to his right hand.

'She made it herself,' said her mother proudly.

'It's very nice, Mini,' he said, making her smile.

Then she performed the same ceremony on his friend. But as she was tying the knot, the *rakhi* fell off its band. Seeing the disappointment on her face, the friend quickly said that the braided colourful band made for a nice *rakhi* too.

'I can stick it back,' said Mini, and stood up to fetch some glue.

'Why don't you tie the other *rakhi* I got?' suggested her father.

'That's OK. I like the braided threads. It's like a friendship band,' said the friend.

Mini fetched her glue bottle and the lotus *rakhi*, but seeing everyone's appreciation of the lotus *rakhi* she ecided to tie it. At first the grip felt very tight but loosened almost immediately.

'So, where are your parents from?' asked Mini's mother to their neighbour's friend as she served them *puris* and *chole*.

'My parents are no more but I have a sister about the same age as Mini and she lives with our Aunt and Uncle in Basera.'

The Tiger Man

A folktale from Manipur, retold by Kanika Sharma

Not so long ago, when the sky was at its bluest, and the forest at its greenest, all creatures could dream of becoming human. The trees, the birds, the smallest bug that still crawls on your back, all tried to make this transformation, but it was still remarkably rare, and extremely difficult.

One day, a most amazing thing happened. The oldest tree in the greenest forest—the top of which had never been seen—turned into a short, stout, old woman. Her breathing still sounded like the rustling of dead leaves, and her eyes resembled crow's feet, which had scratched her branches for so long. Her face was covered in wrinkles of spider webs, making it was impossible to tell her smile from her frown.

When she saw her reflection on water, she screamed in alarm. She had waited patiently, for years, decades, even centuries to become a beautiful woman, and her dream had turned into a nightmare. Knowing not what to do, she started helplessly scratching her face.

Suddenly the reflection of her face grew more wrinkly, and then disappeared completely. The pond rippled, and the Granny Tree looked up to see the prettiest girl she had ever seen. The Granny Tree decided to follow her. They passed a brook, and climbed down one hill, and after a while a village approached, and the Prettiest Girl walked towards it, with the Granny Tree following.

From a distance, the Granny Tree noticed one house in particular. It was a most peculiar house, with no windows and only one huge gigantic door, without any handles. From the look of it, the door could never be opened from the outside.

The Prettiest Girl walked straight for the house, and when she knocked on the door, instead of the treasures of the world the Granny Tree had expected, she saw the girl's seven brothers, standing in a row, according to their height and age. The girl entered the house, leaving the Granny Tree alone.

For the first time, she felt hunger, fatigue, awe and immense envy at the Prettiest Girl—things her wooden brain refused to understand, for it had remained that of a tree. She decided that she would go no further. And next to the seven brother's house, she built a hut.

Years passed, and it was time for the Prettiest Girl to get married. The brothers, not being very rich, decided that the only way to marry her into a good family was to go hunting for treasure. But they had heard that the Tiger Man was roaming in the region.

The people of the village still talk of the Tiger Man—he had been the most ugly man in the whole wide world. Children made fun of him behind his back, grown men called him hideous, and women—ah women—they loathed his very sight. But all the poor man wanted was a woman for a wife, and a man for a friend. But he knew that no man or woman would fill those holes in his heart. So, broken and lonely, the man left the realm, and roamed the forests, the seas, and the desert.

By the time he returned to the hills, he had shed his human form, and taken the face of the wild lord. Yes, creatures turned into men at this time, but not the other way around. But he couldn't bear being a man anymore, and had turned himself into a monster. He had become the Tiger Man.

And so, the seven brothers were afraid to leave their dear sister alone in the house.

They told the Prettiest Girl that she was to open the house for nobody, because the house could not be entered from the outside. But she said, 'What if it is you? When you return, how will I know my brothers are home?'

The youngest and shortest of the brothers came up with an idea. He said, 'Do not open the door for anyone, unless they recite this rhyme—

Loved be, beloved sister.
The jewel and gem mirror each other.
What is once lost is now treasured.
Open the door to regain thy brothers.'

Making sure that the Prettiest Girl had memorized it, the seven brothers embarked on their journey.

A long time passed. The Granny Tree became more bent and crooked. For so long, she was the mightiest tree in the greenest forest, but now, the Granny Tree had grown into an insufferable, jealous hag. She hated the Prettiest Girl, and was jealous of her brothers, her house, and most of all, her youth.

The Tiger Man had not been in the area when the brothers left, but all this time later, he had strolled into the village. He hunted for prey that night, and stopped at the Granny Tree's door. The Granny Tree, seeing the Tiger Man, quivered with fear. The Tiger Man roared at her, and she shrunk into her house.

From there, meek and shaking, she said, 'Please don't eat me, oh Lord Beast, I am but an old woman. My skin is tough and wrinkly, and my flesh is lean. Go next door. A young girl lives there, and she is all alone. It will be the prettiest meal you have ever had.'

And so the Tiger Man stood at the door that could not be opened, and knocked, and pounded on it. But he had no rhyme, so the door remained shut.

But standing there, something moved the Tiger Man. What stood on the other side of the door had brought back snatches of the Tiger Man's earlier, human incarnation. The only thing he wanted was for that door to open, so he could lay his eyes on the Prettiest Girl.

The Tiger Man continued to knock on the door—reduced to begging the girl now. But the door stayed shut.

The Granny Tree meanwhile, unable to sleep, had come out to check whether her evil trick had worked. Her wicked, wooden heart decided to help him. The Granny Tree and the Tiger Man hatched a plan.

The Granny Tree walked up to the door, and asked for some salt. She had run out, and it was too late to go too far. Being kind, the Prettiest Girl opened the tiniest bit of the door, and held out a handful of salt for her. Immediately, the Tiger Man let out a terrible roar, burst into the house and stole the Prettiest Girl into the heart of the forest.

In the greenest forest, the Tiger Man treated the Prettiest Girl as his queen. He hunted the fattest animals for her, fetched her the sweetest honey, and built her the nicest cottage that could be built in the middle of a forest. But she was never allowed to leave it, and her feet were always tied to the strongest pillar. The Prettiest Girl felt imprisoned, and pined for her brothers.

Several years after leaving for their hunt for treasure, the seven brothers finally returned to the village. On arriving home, they discovered their beloved sister was missing. For weeks they searched, rummaged and ransacked the hills in the hope of finding their sister.

Finally, they approached the forest, and found the cottage. They hid in the foliage, and when the Tiger Man left to go hunting, they rushed in, and were overjoyed to find their sister.

Relieved and ecstatic at their return, the sister told them the story of her abduction. They decided that they would kill the Tiger Man. But the Prettiest Girl warned them that he was the strongest creature to have walked, and would easily defeat them all. So they suggested that she run away with them, at once. But she was too scared to run away. She said, 'If the Tiger Man finds me missing, he will never stop looking for me. He will go to every doorstep in every house in the whole wide world looking for me. And when he finds me, he will kill us all.'

The brothers then came up with a plan to trick the Tiger Man. They convinced their sister to pretend to have fallen in love with him, and treat him with the softest kindness she could. They would come back exactly a week later, and on that morning, she was to ask her husband to fill a bamboo pole with water, and bring it for her.

Meanwhile, in the village, the seven brothers decided to take vengeance upon the Granny Tree. They killed her, and a week later, took the old-tree-lady's skin with them to the cottage in the greenest forest.

After a week of fussing over the Tiger Man, and pretending to be besotted with him, the Prettiest Girl woke up in the morning, and said, 'Jewel of my eye, I am craving the sweet water of the stream. Will you please go and fill this bamboo pole with water?'

At the stream, the Tiger Man huffed and puffed, but every time he tried to fill the bamboo pole, the water would pour out of the other side. However hard he tried, and he tried many times, he couldn't do it.

As planned, the seven brothers ran into the cottage as soon as the Tiger Man left and untied the Prettiest Girl from her shackles. They placed the Granny Tree's skin on her bed, and to the foot of the skin, they tied the shackle back. And then they burnt the cottage down.

A crow had tried to tell the Tiger Man of the goings on in his cottage, but he had been too busy filling his bamboo pole, and brushed it aside. For a week his beloved had been the sweetest, most caring woman he could ever imagine, and nothing would give him as much pleasure as fulfilling such a simple wish.

Hours later, when the Tiger Man, frustrated, and miserable, decided to give up and return to his cottage, it was too late. He found nothing and no one there—just ash, swivelling around in the air like the snowflakes of winter. He turned the piles of ash up and down, and looked under every solid thing in the embers, and finally he found it—the burnt skin of an old lady he took to be the Prettiest Girl.

After that, the Tiger Man was never seen in the hills. He never left the forest, or harmed another creature again.

Black Rain

Raja SG

Every year, during Rakshabandhan, Rohit's parents would invite his aunts and uncles from out of town and that would mean a sleepover for them and his cousins. Twelve-year-old Rohit didn't mind sharing his room or sleeping on a mattress on the floor. After a sumptuous dinner and lots of desserts, cooked by his aunts, it was tradition for his cousins to gather around their youngest uncle and listen to his stories from all over the world. This year however, his uncle was abroad on work and couldn't make it back on time, so Rohit's oldest cousin took up the storyteller's role.

'Everyone ready for a story?' announced his seventeen-year old cousin, Ashish.

Rohit cheered in excitement and gathered around him with the others. Ashish sat on the bed while the others took to the floor around it.

'This is a story about a brother and sister,' began Ashish. 'And their names are Rohan and Juhi.'

***

I

Rohan, had turned twelve a month ago and his grandfather gifted him and his five-year-old sister, Juhi, a black Welsh pony that he named Tookie.

'There is something very sinister about him,' their mother had said when Tookie arrived on a day of heavy thunderstorms and rains, not typical for the middle of summer in Central India.

A week later, when his Grandfather passed away in his sleep, after much coaxing, crying, reassuring, and promising, his mother decided not to give Tookie away and build a stable in the estate, a few hundred metres away from their Haveli.

Tookie was two-years-old with a shiny, solid black coat and turned heads everywhere he went, sniffing everything and everyone he met on the grounds. Juhi swore that he would greet her every morning with a smile and friendly dance around her.

But like his mistress, he was terrified of thunderstorms, and would neigh all night, stamping his hoofs on the floor of his musty stable.

Rohan was tall for his age, a little lanky but strong. His thick black hair kept falling on his forehead almost covering his eyes and despite his mother's constant nagging, he would visit the barber once every few months.

II

One night, while their father was away, Rohan was awakened by the sound of thunder, his eyes flinching in the sudden flash of lightening, his hands desperately searching for the comforter, pulling at it to cover his eyes and ears.

The wind made a shrill whistle as it found its way through narrow cracks in the window and dodged the rain slashing over the glass.

Rohan dozed off again, thinking about his pony, only to be awakened by someone pulling at his comforter and calling his name softly. Squinting and pleading more hours of sleep, his eyes opened slightly to see the silhouette of his five-year-old sister Juhi. She had the same dark eyes as her brother and a pointed but smaller nose on a wheatish round face. It was usual for her to crawl into his bed during thunderstorms, and Rohan did not mind that, but he did mind her bringing along her stuffed toys, an elephant, and a monkey that she had named 'Rohan', much to his disapproval. Juhi did not place the monkey next to him, like she always did, but instead curled up to her older brother and hugged him.

'I'm scared,' she whispered.

Rohan patted her forehead and then turned to his left, his back towards her. The thunder continued and his mind wandered to the city, where his father would be packing to take the train back early in the morning. He hoped he could make it home in this weather.

'Do you think papa can come back tomorrow?' asked Juhi.

Rohan shrugged, surprised that she was thinking about the same thing. Lately, their father had missed all their events, the annual day in school, parents day where both won prizes at the science show, and even sports day where Rohan won a championship, acing athletics and discus. But their mother had promised he would come tomorrow and take them for a picnic.

Lightening struck twice in a row and Rohan felt Juhi's grip around his arm tighten.

'Do you think Tookie is OK?' she asked just as Rohan's mind wandered to the stables. 'He is all alone,' she added, her voice quivering.

There was another flash of lightning followed by loud thunder and a trailing neigh.

'Did you hear that?' said Rohan turning around.

Juhi nodded, surprised that it sounded close to their room. Rohan wriggled out of her arm and walked towards the window. Juhi followed holding her doll in one hand and a pillow in another. She wiped the frost on the window and cupped her hands, peering through the glass.

'Oh no,' she cried. 'There he is . . . near the garden gate. Can we pleeease let him in . . . pleeeeeese?'

'Mother will be very cross,' said Rohan, shaking his head.

'But she is sleeping. We can wake up in the morning and let him out before she finds out.'

'No . . . we can't do that. He'll eat all the flowers and poop all over the place. But I should take him back to his stable. It is not safe for him to be out in the rains like this.'

'Can I come with you?'

'No.'

'Please! Please,' begged Juhi. 'I just want to say good night to him.'

'Alright, but wear one of my sweaters.'

Rohan knew where the maid hid the kitchen keys and with those they let themselves out in the wet and dark path leading up to the garden's entrance. It was drizzling outside.

'Hurry, Juhi,' said Rohan and tugged at her. But she wouldn't move.

'What happened?' he asked impatiently, but she stood still as Rohan shut the kitchen door.

Her eyes were fixated at something at a distance, her feet seemed stuck in the mud. Rohan turned to look and froze. Both brother and sister stood still, drops of rain trickling down their faces.

'And where do you think you are going?' said an old man standing in front of the garden gate, his face hidden by shadows and darkness. 'Go back to the house at once, before the black rains begin.'

The man wore a familiar brown sweater, waved his cane in an equally familiar manner and sounded just like their grandfather. Rohan took a step back and brushed against Juhi. He pulled her towards him and began twisting the knob on the door. Juhi was crying holding on to her brother and calling for her mother, as Rohan kept pulling and pushing at the door, the knob not budging from its position. They were locked out.

III

He looked back and felt a sudden gush of cool breeze brush past his face, beads of sweat forming on his forehead, but the old man was nowhere in sight. It was just Tookie neighing and stamping his foot in warning, pushing at the gate with his nose. Rohan kept twisting the knob when he heard a screeching sound from behind. The garden gate swung open and Tookie trotted in, following the path around the garden.

'Stop! Stop!' cried Rohan but Tookie kept going along the haveli and disappeared, with brother and sister running after him. Rohan held on to Juhi and hurried towards the front entrance, ringing the bell and thumping on the door.

'Ma . . . Ma . . . open the door, it's us,' he shouted but the wind blew away his pleas. He wasn't sure if her deep sleep was the reason she couldn't hear them or the fact that her bedroom was in the farthest part of the haveli.

'Where is she? Why is she not opening the door?' cried Juhi.

Rohan wiped her tears with his sleeves and kept banging at the door. But the door didn't open, their mother didn't take them in her arms, and the rains didn't stop. Rohan's face looked pale, his mind racing through thoughts, none of them making sense to him. Finally, he gave up on the door and hurriedly walked towards the main road.

'Where are we going?' asked a Juhi.

'To Goel Uncle's house,' he replied.

The Goels were their closest neighbors about a mile down the road. Juhi wanted to say 'No', but she trusted her brother's judgment and held on to his arm, keeping up with his pace.

'Don't worry Juhi, don't cry,' consoled Rohan, his voice shaking.

Drenched in sweat and rain, they walked as fast as they could but Goel Uncle's house seemed farther away than they had imagined.

IV

'Can you run?' whispered Rohan as he took a step back. Juhi nodded tightening her grip on his hand.

Turning around, they ran, Rohan pulling Juhi along, not looking back once, not caring about the puddles of water on the road, the broken twigs and leaves, their only saviour, the full moon and the wet road glistening in its light. They just needed to get to the Goel House. They kept running, panting, and sweating but not stopping for one moment, following the road wherever it would take them.

Suddenly, they heard a reassuring neigh ahead and hastened their pace to catch up with it. The road curved sharply to the right and they were about to take the turn, when two lights appeared out of nowhere blinding them. All they heard was a loud screeching and skidding sound.

Months later, the local newspaper flashed a story of unusual sightings in the vicinity of the *haveli* where many residents complained of hearing neighs and spotting two young children, a boy and girl walking down the road in the middle of the night, holding hands. No one had been able to see their faces but some said the little girl looked back at them and smiled, her teeth glistening in the moonlight.

***

There was pin drop silence in the room and Ashish had a big grin on his face. His younger cousins seemed to be deep in thought. Reaching out under the pillow he pressed a button on a toy. There was a loud neigh and Rohit and his cousins jumped up in surprise. But realizing what had just happened, they burst out laughing. Rohit was just glad that he wasn't going to sleep alone in his room that night.

A Pinprick

An ancient Bengali tale

On a hill on the shore of the mighty sea was a tiny old hut. A brother and sister lived in it, without their parents, who had died in a storm many years ago. Having no money, the brother had to go fishing in the sea for food, and everyday he came back with two fish—one for him and one for his sister.

One morning, the brother had a stroke of luck. He chanced upon a school of hilsa and caught them all. He rushed to the market and sold all his fish, not forgetting, of course, to keep one for himself and one for his beloved sister.

His sister was over the moon, wanting to cook them right there and then. But the brother had to go out in the afternoon to bring back the nets he had left on the beach. Asking her to cook the fish for dinner, the brother left.

All afternoon, the sister cooked the fish. She marinated them in *haldi* and *sarson*. She heated the oil, and fried them.

She then prepared the light gravy that would go so well with the fish. Just as she finished, and was about to start cooking the rice, there was a knock on the door. It was a grey, old man wearing bright saffron ropes.

Pagla Rishi (mad sage) had not eaten in days. He had walked all the way from Tarapeet, and had not stopped for water or food. No one knew why the Rishi was walking, and no one had asked, knowing his answer would not be to their question but to some other question from some other time, asked by someone else. Pagla Rishi offered no answer to people who asked him questions, and he had no questions for people who could give him answers. So people rarely spoke to him and that is why they called him mad.

The sister opened the door slowly, not sure what to make of this strange-looking man in saffron rags, rarely having left her hut, and never having heard of Pagla Rishi. But she had heard of the powers of the Rishis that walked around the world, and she didn't want to make him angry. The Rishi looked thirsty, and the sister offered him water. The Rishi looked tired, so she offered him rest. He looked hungry, so she offered him food. But the Rishi said nothing and simply walked into the hut.

Inside, the Rishi drank up all the water, but he did not speak. He then slept for an hour, waking up with his stomach growling. So the sister gave him both the fish she had so lovingly prepared for her brother. But he still did not speak. After he had eaten, she told him her story, about how she and her brother were orphaned, how her young brother had to go out fishing. How she would stay back at home, looking out of the tiny window of her tiny hut at the endless ocean, waiting for him to return. And yet, the Rishi did not speak.

As Pagla Rishi was leaving, he turned to the sister, and smiled.

'Your water has quenched my thirst, and your bed has given me rest. Your food has made me strong, as after walking so long, I was weak. And your story, dear girl . . . your story has moved me. For this kindness, I will give you gifts that will make you rich and keep you smiling forever. Every day, when you comb your hair, pearls will fall from it. And every day, when you wash your hands, prawns will fall from the water. And every time you dry your hands, your towel will fill with the most beautiful flowers in the land.'

As soon as he was gone, the sister combed her hair. And she washed her hands, and then dried them. From the comb pearls cascaded on to the floor! She would never be poor again. She washed her hands, and from the water appeared prawns the size of her fist! She would never be hungry again. Then she dried her hands, and she found roses and orchids and lilies that filled her heart with joy.

But then she remembered her brother, who would soon come home from the beach, and demand his hilsa. She quickly picked the four biggest prawns that had appeared in the water, and cooked them with the sweetest coconut milk. She scattered the flowers and pearls around the hut, making it gleam and radiate with beauty. And then she waited for her brother to return.

When the brother walked into the house, he was shocked.

Seeing the pearls, he asked, 'Where did you steal all these from?'

And on seeing the flowers, his anger growing, he asked, 'Which man came to my house to give you these flowers?'

And on seeing his meal, he flew into a rage, convinced she had stolen the prawns from another poor fisherman. 'Who did you get these fish from?'

The sister, still overjoyed, happily explained what happened, not affected by her brother's wrath. On hearing the story, the brother's anger subsided, and transformed into glee. She had done it! They did not need to live in their little hut by the beach. He didn't need to go out and fish in the hot sun all day. They were finally free!

Immediately, the brother decided what he had to do. He would go to the city, find the palace, and meet the young king. He would tell him of his sister's story and the king would be amazed.

He set out for the city. When he reached, he sought an audience with the young king, and after days of waiting, he finally got it. He sold some of the pearls he had brought with him and bought the nicest clothes he had ever worn. With his head held high, he walked into the palace to tell the king his story.

The young king's reaction baffled him. The king wanted to meet his sister immediately, he had been looking for a wife—and a girl who could produce pearls from her hair, prawns by washing her hands, and flowers just by drying them—who better to be queen of his realm? Overjoyed, the brother asked for a king's guard to be sent for his sister. The guard left the very next morning and, after riding for three days on horseback, reached the hut.

The sister, unsure of what to make of the situation, and more than a little nervous at making such a long journey, decided to trust the guard. She left at the crack of dawn the next day, and rode on his horse, mile after mile.

After hours of riding, the sister grew tired. They were near a river, and she asked for the guard to help her down so she could drink some water. Unknown to her, a *dayini*, or witch, stood amidst the trees, watching the girl freshen up. And, lo and behold, she saw beautiful pearls fall from her hair when she combed it, and prawns leap from the river when she washed her hands, and a shower of flowers fall from her *gamcha*, as she dried her hands!

The *dayini* rubbed her hands together in greed on seeing the pearls, and smacked her lips at the prawns, and sighed at the beauty of the flowers. Then she hatched a plan.

The sister was ready to leave, when the witch appeared out of the foliage disguised as a sweet little girl. The sister bent down to hug the girl. Suddenly the witch produced a pin, which she stuck into the sister's head.

In a snap, the sister turned into a little sparrow, and the witch turned into the sister.

With great pomp and glory, the witch appeared at the king's court disguised as the sister. She pretended to be happy to see her brother (whom she couldn't recognize at first). And she bent in curtsy before the king. The king looked at her and was immediately taken by her, but first he asked her to show him her powers.

The witch asked for a comb, a bowl of water and a towel, which were produced immediately by the courtiers. Then, the witch picked up the comb and brushed her long, black hair, and . . .

Nothing happened.

She washed her hands, and still nothing happened! She

dried them, rubbing the towel violently against her hand, and still nothing happened.

The king was furious. He immediately sent the witch to the stables, where she would have to work for the rest of her life. As for the brother, he ordered for him to be put to death in three day's time, on *amaabarsha*, the night of the new moon.

Far away, the next morning, the sister-sparrow sat on the porch of a house, nibbling on some rice grains the women of the house had dropped there. As she was eating, sad and lonely, and worried about her brother, she overheard the women talking about a man who had claimed to have a sister fit to marry the king. The sister had turned out to be ugly and untalented, and so the poor man was to be put to death in two day's time.

The sister-sparrow panicked. Lifting herself out of her gloom, she flew as fast as she could, into the city she had never visited before. For hours, she searched for the palace. Then she spotted a huge building with a beautiful garden, where a handsome man was strolling.

The sister sang the most beautiful song a sparrow has ever sung. The man, mesmerized walked as fast as he could towards her. It was a sparrow's song, but seeing that it was human once, the words seemed to make sense to him.

He heard a story of such woe, and yet oddly familiar, that he at once ordered his courtiers to come out and hear it. All the courtiers heard of the lost brother, the wicked *dayini*, and how a poor girl had been showered with extraordinary gifts. The sparrow told them that she still had the *dayini's* pin from days ago, and how she had carried it under her feathers.

The king approached the sparrow and held her in his hands. Below her breast, lay a single, sharp pin. At once, he ordered the imposter-sister to appear before him. As soon as she arrived, he pricked the pin on her temple. Almost at once, the sparrow he was holding turned into the most beautiful woman he had seen, and the imposter turned into an ugly witch.

The king ordered the brother to be brought in front of him. But before freeing him, the king demanded to see the miracles the sister apparently could perform. The comb, the bowl of water and the towel were placed in front of her.

As soon as she touched the comb to her hair, pearls showered down, like raindrops from a dark sky. When she immersed her hands in the bowl, four large prawns fit only for a king popped out of it. Then she dried her hands in the towel, and threw the towel at the king, and he was showered with the most beautiful flowers that had ever blossomed in his realm.

The king ordered the brother's chains to be unshackled and slapped on the witch. He announced to his court, and his kingdom that there was to be a wedding, and they were to have the most beautiful queen that any kingdom had ever seen.

That is how the brother became the king's most trusted consul and companion, the sister the queen of all his lands, and the evil *dayini* lay dead on an *amaabarsha* night.

All about Rakhi and Bhai Dooj

Rakhi: The Thread of Love

Subhamoy Das

Rakshabandhan, or Rakhi, is a special day in the Hindu calendar, marked by the full moon in the month of *Shravan*. It is a day to celebrate the special bond between brothers and sisters, signified by the sister tying a sacred thread, or *rakhi* on the right hand of the brother.

Bonds and Protects

Rakshabandhan literally means 'a bond of protection', when a sister prays for the long life of her brother, and in return, the brother vows to forever protect the sister. *Rakhis* are ideally made of silk with gold and silver threads, beautifully crafted embroidered sequins, and studded with semi-precious stones.

A *rakhi* may not always be shared just between a brother and sister. In fact, when a *rakhi* is tied on the wrists of close friends and neighbours, it also signifies a bond of protection, and a life of peace and co-existence. Festivals such as Rakhi have always helped ease tensions—between siblings, families, and in fact whole communities.

The Auspicious Full Moon

In Northern India, the full moon night of Rakshabandhan or Rakhi Purnima is also called Kajri Purnima or Kajri Navami, when wheat or barley is sown, and goddess Bhagwati is worshipped. In Western Indian states, the festival is called Nariyal Purnima or the Coconut Full Moon. In Southern India, it is known as Shravan Purnima, which is an important religious occasion.

The Many Names of Rakhi

Rakshabandhan is known by various names: Vish Tarak—the destroyer of venom, Punya Pradayak—the bestower of boons, and Pap Nashak—the destroyer of sins. All these names underscore the real significance of this joyful festival.

Rakhi Legends from Hindu Mythology

Subhamoy Das

Hindu mythology, including the Puranas, the *Ramayana* and the *Mahabharata* speak of the Rakhi as a bonding and unifying power, and symbolizing all aspects of protection of good from evil forces.

Varuna and Rakhi

Rakhi was originally intended to be a ritual offering for the sea-god Lord Varuna, says one mythological tale. So, devotees offer coconuts and flowers to Varuna, and ceremonial bathing and fairs at waterfronts are held on the day of Rakshabandhan. This tradition of worshipping Varuna during the Rakhi festival is popular especially in Western India.

Indra and Rakhi

According to another mythological legend, when Lord Indra, the King of the Heavens, was unable to cope with the constant attacks waged by Daitya Raja, the Demon King, he sought the advice of Devaguru Brihaspati, the Guru of the Gods. Upon Brihaspati's advice, Indra's wife, Indrani, tied a *rakhi* on Indra's wrist, on the auspicious occasion of Shravan Purnima. It is said that the *rakhi* gave Indra the power to vanquish the Demon King. Thus the sacred silken thread helped Indra regain control over his celestial empire.

Yama and Rakhi

Even Yama, the Lord of Death, is said to have observed Rakshabandhan. His sister Yamuna had tied the *rakhi* on Yama's wrist amidst worship and rituals. Deeply touched by her sister's love, Yama granted her immortality. So, it is believed that a *rakhi* tied by a sister on the day of Rakshabandhan can protect a brother from sudden death.

Yudhishthir and Rakhi

In the great epic *Mahabharata*, we find Lord Krishna advising King Yudhishthir, the eldest of the Pandava brothers, to tie a *rakhi* to guard himself against impending evils and protection from the perils of the great war of Kurukshetra. Yudhisthir is said to have observed the ceremony of the Rakshabandhan and tied the sacred thread around his own wrist. Stories from the *Mahabharata* also mention about Kunti, the mother of the Pandavas, tying a *rakhi* on her grandson Abhimanyu. It is also said that Draupadi, the wife of the Pandavas, observed Rakshabandhan by presenting the sacred *rakhi* to Lord Krishna.

Bali, Vishnu, Lakshmi and Rakhi

In the mythological tales from the *Puranas*, we find the beautiful legend of Bali, grandson of the great Vishnu devotee Prahalad. Lord Vishnu was so impressed by the might of Bali, that he promised him divine protection and immortality until Bali was crowned the King. As the legend goes, Vishnu left Vaikunth, his abode in the heavens, and started guarding Bali's kingdom. Vishnu's wife, Goddess Lakshmi, was alarmed at her husband's action and decided to bring the Lord back to heaven. Lakshmi disguised herself as a Brahmin woman and went to Bali to seek protection till her husband returned. He welcomed her into his palace. As the occasion of Shravana Purnima dawned, Lakshmi tied a *rakhi* on Bali's wrist. Bali was greatly touched by this gesture and asked her what she wanted as a gift. Lakshmi then revealed her real identity and asked Bali to let go of her husband Vishnu. Bali promised to keep his words on the condition that the couple should visit his palace every year on Rakshabandhan.

Since then, people say, it has been a tradition to invite sisters over to their brother's place on Shravan Purnima to celebrate the occasion with a feast. So, this festival of Rakshabandhan is also called 'Baleva' after King Bali's legendary devotion. Even till this day, sisters ceremonially recite this verse from the Puranas while tying the *rakhi*:

Yena baddho Balee raajaa daanavendro mahaabalah
tena twaam anubadhnaami rakshe maa chala maa chala

'I am tying a *rakhi* on you, like the one on mighty demon king Bali.
Be firm, O *rakhi*, do not falter.'

Rakhi Tales from Indian History

Subhamoy Das

Did you know that the strong bond of Rakhi gave rise to numerous political ties among kingdoms and princely states? The pages of Indian history testify that Rajput and Maratha queens have sent *rakhis* even to Mughal kings who, despite their differences, have assuaged their '*rakhi*-sisters' by offering help and protection at critical moments, honouring the bond of Rakhi. Even matrimonial alliances have been established between kingdoms through the exchange of *rakhis*.

Alexander the Great

The oldest known historical event associated with Rakshabandhan occurred when Alexander the Great embarked upon invading the Indian subcontinent in 326 BC. Alexander was confronted by King Porus, the brave ruler of the North-Western region. History has it that Alexander's wife approached Porus with a *rakhi*, in the form of a simple sacred thread to ensure the safety of her husband. She tied a *rakhi* on his hand, prior to the battle, urging him not to hurt her husband. Porus graciously accepted the *rakhi* and refrained from striking Alexander. Such has been the power of *rakhi*!

Emperor Humayun

In the 16th century, the queen of Chittoor, Rani Karnavati presented a *rakhi* to emperor Humayun to seek allegiance and military assistance from the mighty Mughal empire. The *rakhi* helped the kingdom of Chittoor from being annexed by the Sultan of Gujarat. Humayan was deeply touched by the friendly gesture of the queen and ordered his forces to protect Chittor from the invaders. Although the Mughal army marched towards Chittoor to help the distressed Karnavati, it was a too late. Humayun may have failed to save the queen and her other Rajput ladies from committing *jauhar* or self immolation, but it was the *rakhi* that even the mighty Mughal emperor couldn't ignore.

Rabindranath Tagore

In 1905, the British Empire decided to divide Bengal on the basis of religion. At that time Rabindranath Tagore, the Noble-laureate poet, used the platform of Rakshabandhan to bring people closer. First, as a protest, he marched into a mosque, and tied *rakhis* on the people praying there. Further, he arranged a ceremony to celebrate Rakshabandhan in order to reinforce the bond of love and togetherness particularly between the Hindus and the Muslims of Bengal.

Bhai Dooj: The Post-Diwali Festival

Subhamoy Das

Nowhere is the bond between brothers and sisters as glorified as in India. Hindus celebrate this special relationship twice every year, with the festivals of Rakshabandhan and Bhai Dooj.

What, When & How

After the high voltage celebrations of Diwali, the festival of lights and fire-crackers, brothers and sisters all over India get ready for Bhai Dooj. Sisters demonstrate their love by putting an auspicious 'tilak' or 'tika'—a dot or mark made of vermilion or sandalwood paste—on the forehead of their brothers and perform the ritual of *aarti* for him by showing him the light of the holy flame. Gifts are exchanged as well.

Bhai Dooj or 'Bhai Tika,' as it's often called, is celebrated on the fifth and last day of Diwali. The name 'Dooj' means the second day after the new moon, the day of the festival, and 'Bhai' means brother.

Myths & Legends

Bhai Dooj is also called Yama Dwiteeya as it's believed that on this day, Yamaraj, the Lord of Death and the Custodian of Hell, visits his sister Yamuna, who puts the auspicious mark on his forehead and prays for his well being. So it's held that anyone who receives a *tilak* from his sister on this day would never be hurled into hell.

According to one legend, on this day, Lord Krishna, after slaying the Narakasura demon, went to his sister Subhadra who welcomed him with lamp, flowers and sweets, and put the holy protective spot on her brother's forehead.

Yet another story is that of Lord Mahavir, the founder of Jainism. When attained nirvana, his brother King Nandivardhan was distressed because he missed him, and was comforted by his sister Sudarshana. Bhai Dooj, according to this story, is a celebration of this love.

Bhai Phonta

In Bengal, Bhai Dooj is called 'Bhai Phonta', which is performed by the sister who fasts until she applies a *phonta* or mark with sandalwood paste on her brother's forehead, offers him sweets and gifts, and prays for his long and healthy life.

Every brother eagerly awaits this occasion as it is an opportunity for a good feast, coupled with an enthusiastic exchange of gifts, and merriment, amidst the sound of conch shells in every Bengali household.

What's Important about Bhai Dooj

Like all other Hindu festivals, Bhai Dooj too has a lot to do with family ties and social attachments. It serves as a good time, especially for children, and for the whole family to share the glee and joys after Diwali.

Sometimes, sisters who are unable to meet their brothers in person, send their 'tika'—the spot of protection—in an envelope by post. Virtual 'tilaks' and Bhai Dooj e-cards have made it even easier for brothers and sisters, who live far away from each other, to greet their siblings on this occasion.

Fun Festival Activities

Make Your Own *Rakhi*

Here's a step-by-step guide to help you make a traditional decorated *rakhi* wrist-band for this Rakshabandhan.

What You Need:

• Strands of silk threads • A pair of scissors • Cotton thread to tie knots • Beads, *sitaras*, golden threads and sponge to decorate • Glue • A toothbrush with hard bristles

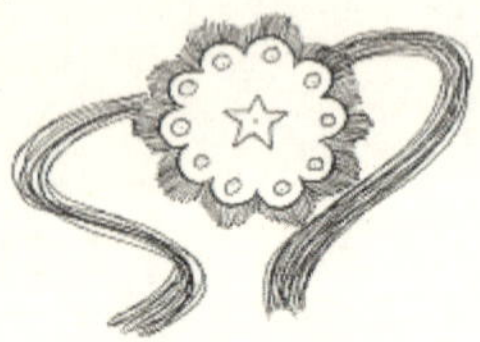

MAKE IT!

1) Take 20 to 24-inch silk thread strands in a bunch. If you want to make multi-coloured *rakhis* take silk threads of different colours.
2) Tie a tight knot with a cotton thread at about the one-fourth mark of the silken thread bunch. The one-fourth part will be made into a *rakhi* while the three-fourth will be the string to tie around the wrist.
3) Now make sure the heads of the silk threads of the one-fourth part of the bunch do not remain in loops, in case they are, cut them with a pair of scissors.
4) Once they are free of loops, rub these threads hard with a toothbrush with strong strokes by holding on to the knot tightly. With repeated strokes, the silk threads turn fluffy and soft.

5) To make the string, divide the three-fourth part of the silk thread in two equal parts and plait them separately. At the end tie a knot and brush again.
6) Once this is done, decorate it with beads or *sitaras*. Stick them with glue.
7) You can also buy a sheet of sponge of a suitable colour, cut it into a star or flower shape, and decorate it with beads. Golden threads can be entwined and used for decoration.

by Subhamoy Das

Safety Pin *Rakhi*

A *rakhi* made from safety pins! And no one will ever guess.

You need:

- 48 Coloured two-inch Safety Pins
- Beads
- One thread of elastic

MAKE IT!

1) Cut two elastic strands of about one foot each. Tie a bead onto each cord to keep pins from falling off.
2) Begin by stringing a closed safety pin onto both cords, one cord through the head of the pin, and one through the loop at the end.
3) String two more safety pins alternating the way the heads face. This will keep the bracelet from getting too big on one side. String a bead on each cord.

4) Continue stringing on three safety pins, a bead; three safety pins, a bead, until it is big enough to go around your brother's wrist.
5) Cut off the first beads, loop around and bring ends together to form the bracelet. Tie them together in a very tight double knot. Trim ends.

String *Rakhi*

A simple *rakhi* that is a breeze to make!

You need:

• Notebook or clipboard (use any flat surface) • Three strands of different-coloured string • Masking tape (use this to tape your *rakhi* down)

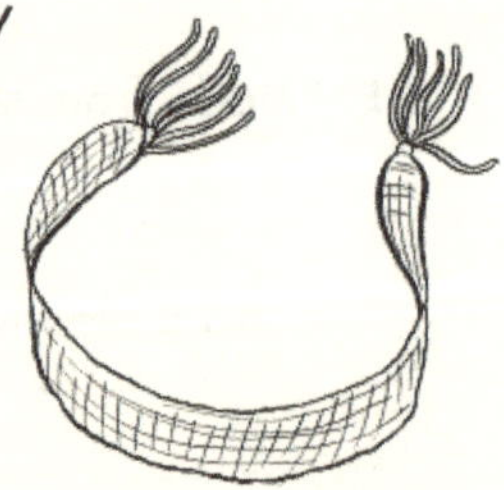

MAKE IT!

1) Match your strands of string, according to their colour.
2) Make sure your bracelet is long enough, measure from the tip of your fingers to your shoulder, then double it.
3) Fold the measured string in half, exactly in the middle.
4) With the fold intact, form a loop at the centre of the threads.
5) Tie an knot at the bottom of the loop, leaving the loop approximately one-inch long.
6) Attach the loop under the clip of the clipboard or tape it to a notebook.

7) Separate the threads in an alternating colour pattern. Using your first string, tie a knot around each of the remaining five strings in order. Your first string is now at the end of the six strings.

8) Repeat with each of the remaining five strings. You should be able to see the pattern emerging at this point.

9) Continue to tie knots until you're left with a couple of inches of unknotted thread.

10) On Rakhi day, tie the unknotted thread around your brother's hand!

Prepare a Rakhi Ceremony

This Rakhi morning, go traditional!

You need:

• A *rakhi* • A silver, brass, or metallic plate • *Tilak* • Rice grains • *Agarbattis* • *Diya* • Sweets • Gifts!

DO IT!

1) On Rakhi morning, prepare a plate with *tilak*, your *rakhi*, rice grains, *agarbattis*, *diyas*, sweets and, of course, your gifts, arranged in a circle.

2) If you are the sister, take the plate, and perform *aarti* by raising the plate to his face (don't get too close!) and making three clockwise circles around his face.

3) Then, put the *tilak* on your brother's forehead, and put some rice grains on it.
4) Now tie the *rakhi*.
5) Feed your brother a bit of the sweet, and have him do the same to you.
6) After that, exchange your gifts, and that, of course, is the best part!

Pocket Wall Hanging

A perfect gift for Rakhi—who doesn't need an extra pocket or two?

You need:

- Colourful waste cloths
- Needle and thread
- A pair of scissors

MAKE IT!

1) Cut out a rectangle the size you want your wall hanging to be out of the cloth.
2) Decide on pocket size. Cut pockets out of the left over fabric. If you are feeling lazy, go ahead and cut out the pockets of an old pair of jeans.
3) Pin them where you want them on the large rectangle. Sew on three sides, with the top of each pocket left open.
4) Sew a piece hang or stick it to the wall with double-sided tape.
5) Your sibling's Pocket Wall Hanging is ready! Fill pockets with supplies, like their favourite pens, keys, etc.

The Story of Your Lives

All you need to really make your sibling's Bhai Dooj!

You need:

• Colourful paper • Pencils • Needle and thread
• Ruler • Colour pencils, crayons • A pair of scissors
• Lots of old memories

MAKE IT!

1) The first thing you need to do is write the story of your lives together. Write about the best memories you have with your siblings, your favourite hobbies, all your favourite foods, your favourite holidays, movies you love watching together, all of it!
2) According to the amount you have written, figure out the size of your book.
3) You will be folding the paper in half and sewing it up the middle, so the paper needs to be twice as long as you want each page to be.
4) Take a ruler and measure a line separating your pages exactly in half. Then place a dot at one-inch intervals so your stitching will be even.
5) Thread enough string so you have three times the line's length. Start at the bottom, leaving four inches of thread for tying a knot when you are finished. Now push the needle through the paper.
6) Go up the book following the line, with big stitches at every dot.

7) Once you reach the top, go back down following the line again. Repeat this one more time.
8) And hey presto! You have made a bound book which your sibling will treasure for the rest of his or her lives!

Spanish Giant Paper Mask

These masks sit on top of your sibling's head and are used often in Spanish carnivals. Now give your own version of this as a beautiful Bhai Dooj gift.

You will need:

• A balloon • Liquid glue • Water • Vaseline • Newspaper • An old tennis ball • Paints • Coloured strips of paper

MAKE IT!

1) Inflate a balloon and tie a knot at the end. Put some petroleum jelly or Vaseline all over the balloon.
2) Make some papier-mache glue by adding equal measures of glue and water.
3) Cover the balloon with the glue you have made and paste some newspaper on it. Do three layers of this.
4) Leave it aside to dry.
5) Once dry, and hard, deflate the balloon (by pricking it with a pin). Pull it out of the shell.
6) Cut an old tennis ball in half, and glue each half on to the shell you have made to make the eyes of the mask.

7) Paint the mask.
8) Paint the half tennis balls to make the eyes. Make a mouth as well with paint.
9) Trim the base of the mask so that it sits on the top of your head. Make little holes on either side of the base of the mask. Attach a piece of elastic in the holes and around your chin, and tie the mask in place over your head. Or you can stick it on to a hair-band.

Photo Project

This is fast becoming an internet phenomenon. People all over the world are photographing one particular thing every day for days, months and even years. This can become the best gift for your sibling this Rakhi. Gift them themselves!

You need:

- Camera
- Computer with Adobe Photoshop
- Your sibling's beautiful face!

MAKE IT!

1) Take a picture of your sibling every morning, as soon as they wake up, or just before they do. It will be nice if you can get the same pose, but if not, just take a 'mug-shot', a shot of their face. Notice any changes in their face?

2) Use a software like Adobe Photoshop and stitch all your photographs together into the coolest photo-collage ever—all you need to do is place the pictures chronologically next to each other.
3) Print out on photographic paper, and if you have time enough before the big day, get your parents to frame it.

Stop-Motion Animation

Does you sibling bore you on normal days? On Rakhi, animate them!

You need:

- A camera
- A computer with Power Point
- Your sibling!

MAKE IT!

1) Stop-Motion animation is much simpler than it sounds, but it is very tedious. An object is moved very slightly between individually photographed frames, giving the illusion of motion.
2) Try it first with a doll. Take a photograph of the doll standing straight.
3) Now move the hand slightly and take another photograph. Turn the hand completely around, taking as many photographs in short intervals along the way.
4) Be careful to take the photographs from the same angle throughout.
5) Put all the photos into a slideshow with less than five

seconds per slide. You will have your first stop-motion animation film!

6) Now, get your sibling to pose. Get him or her to wave at the camera, but to do it very slowly.
7) First get them to raise their arms, then get them to change it very slowly, and take as many snaps at every position, as you can.
8) Put them all together in a slideshow, and you have your very own *Wallace and Gromit*.

Pick-Up-Sticks

A traditional Chinese game for hours of fun!

You need:

• Paints and paintbrushes • 30 thin wooden sticks (you can replace this with plastic straws, but being lighter, the game is much tougher)

MAKE IT!

1) To make your set of pick-up sticks, paint the ends of your 30 wooden sticks with the following colours: one black, three red, five blue, nine green, and twelve yellow.
2) Assign points to each colour as follows: black—ten points, red—five points, blue—three points, green—two points, and yellow—one point.
3) Use a table or the floor to play the game. Hold the sticks upright in a bunch in one hand just above the floor or table. Release the sticks and let them fall. Now try to

remove the sticks one by one without moving any other stick in the pile.

4) You can use the black stick to help you remove other sticks. Now, taking turns, remove sticks from the pile, until you move another by mistake.
5) Once a mistake is made, count the value of your sticks. Keep playing, the first to get to a 100 points is the winner!

It's a Line-Up

A Noughts and Crosses variant that will save you hours of boredom.

You need:

• Paper • Pencils • Two or more players

PLAY IT!

1) Draw a 42-grid square, seven across and six down.
2) The game starts from the bottom of the grid, upwards.
3) The winner is the first to make a horizontal, vertical or diagonal row of four. All other rules remain the same as traditional Noughts and Crosses.

The Great Rakhi Match-Up

Match the siblings!

You need:

- A pencil

DO IT!

Just match the first column of full names with their sibling's first names in the second column!

Dinanath Mangeshkar	Priya
Peter Fonda	Kanimozhi Karunanidhi
Ekta Kapoor	John
Jane Cusack	Priyanka
Sanjay Dutt	Lata
Rahul Gandhi	Tusshaar
M.K. Stalin	Ashmit
Amisha Patel	Maggie
Jake Gyllenhaal	Jane
Charles Lamb	Michael
Janet Jackson	Farhan
Cleopatra	Dinara
Marat Safin	Mary
Zoya Akhtar	Ptolemy

Who Am I?

The perfect game for when all your cousins and family land up for Bhai Dooj.

You need:

• Post-Its • Names of famous people

PLAY IT!

1) Give all the players sheets of Post-Its with names of famous people on them.
2) Each player pastes the Post-It on his/her forehead. Thus, each player knows the identity of every other player, except their own.
3) Each player then asks the group 'yes' or 'no' questions (like 20-Questions). The object of the game is to deduce which famous person you are.
4) Take turns and go around the circle.
5) For the next round, keep your pad of Post-Its ready. Have each person write down one famous person's name and hand it to the person sitting to the right of him or her.
6) Keep going till your cousins need to leave!

Wish like an Egyptian

And we don't mean like a revolutionary, but like an ancient Egyptian!

You need:

• Pen • Paper • Colours

MAKE IT!

1) Have you always wanted to walk, talk and write like an Egyptian? Well, here's taking you a step closer!
2) The formal writing system of the Ancient Egyptians is known as Hieroglyphs. They use pictures and symbols that either refer to a corresponding alphabet, or represent the picture as a whole. Thus, a picture of a bird could refer to a bird itself, but also to the alphabet A. Here are some basic Egyptian letters:

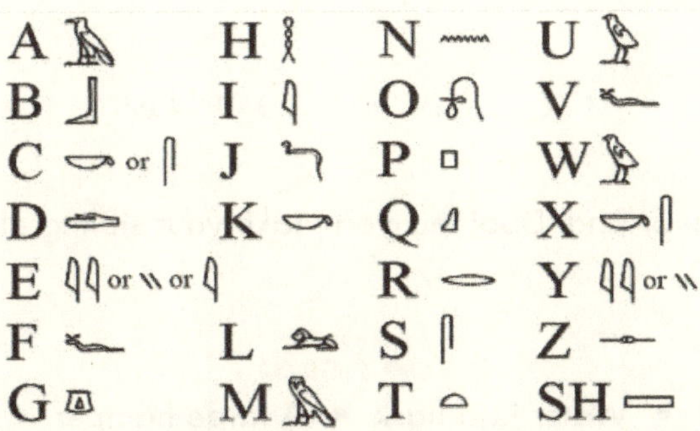

3) Now put down your Rakhi wish in Egyptian, and make sure to give your sibling this chart, so he or she can decipher your wish. What's the point otherwise?

String Pictures

A beautiful gift for Rakhi!

You need:

• Stiff card • Pencil • Thin brush • Coloured strings of wool • Soft cloth

MAKE IT!

1) Cut a piece of card paper.
2) Lightly sketch out a picture with the pencil. Draw only the outlines—trees, flowers, animals . . .
3) Brush glue over the pencil lines.
4) Now stick on the strings of wool neatly over glue marks.
5) Press down firmly with a cloth.
6) Hang up your picture if you like or make a card with it.

Get a Picnic Together

For Rakhi or Bhai Dooj this year, take your sibling along for a picnic!

You need:

• Food • Water in a flask • A large hamper • Paper plates and cups • Napkins • Spoons and forks • Tin/bottle opener • Serving spoons • Dusters • Mats or durries to sit on • Games—football, playing cards etc.

DO IT!

1) Food: Choose stuff that won't go squishy, soggy, watery or bad in a short time. Pack different things in different lunch boxes or plastic bags. On them write what's inside with a pen—sandwiches, stuffed rotis, kathis, pizzas for solid eating and munchies such as chips, nuts, crispies, roasted *channa*, cheese cubes and fruit for snacking. That makes it easier to take out only what you want at a time, rather than turn everything out. Also pack salt and pepper, sauce and soft drinks. Sauce packets that come with home delivered pizzas are great.
2) Water: in a flask.
3) Pack everything in a large hamper. Always take more food than you need—picnics make you ravenous.
4) Also pack paper plates, paper cups, napkins, spoons for serving and eating, knife, tin/bottle opener and dusters.
5) Durries or mats to sit on.
6) Games: football, cricket, skipping rope, playing cards, any other game you like. Paper and pencil for games and notes.
7) Binoculars, for bird-watching.
8) Old newspapers for sitting on, for wrapping rubbish or to keep the sun off!
9) Sunhats
10) A few clothes pegs to hold down paper napkins and other fly-away things.
11) A big garbage bag to dump litter like empty cans, leftover food, peels.
12) Got it together? Now go. What are you waiting for?

Staircase

Another fun game to play with your cousins when they come visiting!

You need:

• Pens/pencils • Paper • Dictionary (optional)

PLAY IT!

1) Any number of players can play. Let the players use a dictionary, unless they want to test their vocabulary.
2) All the players have five minutes to write down a list of nine words beginning with the same letter.
3) The point is that each word must be one-letter longer than the last and the first word must be two letters long.
4) Players score a point for a two-letter word, two points for a three-letter word and so on up to nine for a ten-letter word. The player with the highest score is the winner.

Be
Bet
Bean
Brand
Barber
Brighter
Beetroot
Bandicoot
Bamboozled
Blasphemous

D, A, B, G,H, I, L, M, N, O, S, T are easy letters to start with.
E, F, J, K, P, R, U and Y are more difficult.
C, Q, V, X and Z are almost impossible.

Battleships

Fighting with your siblings all the time? Now it's your turn to destroy them in this fun game for two.

You need:

• Paper • Pencils/pens

MAKE IT!

1) Draw a grid of 144 squares numbering the squares across 1, 2, 3 and so on and lettering them down a, b, c, d and so on.
2) Each player then deploys his/her navy of six war vessels by shading in the squares they are going to occupy.
   This is what each player has:

1 battleship:	5 squares
1 cruiser:	4 squares
2 destroyers:	3 squares each
1 corvette:	2 squares
1 submarine:	1 square

3) The game starts after each player has shaded in his or her six vessels using eighteen squares.

4) The players now take turns to call out a square b-8, e-10 and so on. If the square that has been called out happens to be part of the other player's vessels, he or she must admit that he or she has been hit and say which of his or her vessels has been hit.
5) He or she must also cross out the square that has been hit.
6) The first player to sink his or her opponent's entire fleet is the winner.

Limerick your Gift

Get away by giving your siblings something nice and cheap!

You need:

• Pen • Paper • Your imagination!

DO IT!

1) There was a poet called Edward Lear who made limericks very popular, though people had been writing them much earlier. They have five lines. The first two lines rhyme with each other and with the fifth line, while the third and the fourth lines rhyme with each other.
2) The first line usually begins 'There was a young (or old) man or woman (or boy or girl) of somewhere'. Then you think of a rhyme for the second line. That gives you an idea for the last line. There are two short lines in between.

For instance:

There was a young boy from New Delhi
Who had such an enormous belly
That he was able
To use it as a table,
When it wasn't wobbling like jelly!

Complete these limerick by filling in the blanks with your own ideas and words.

There was an alien from Outer Space
Who said, 'I want to go to a place
Where there are ....
And ....
This planet is such a disgrace!

Now all you need to do is write one with your brother or sister in it!

Pillow Pack

A great gift-wrapping idea!

You need:

• Ivory paper/chart paper • Pencils
• Ruler • A pair of scissors
• Knitting needle/paintbrush
• Adhesive • Sequins • Lace

MAKE IT!

1) Pillow packs are best for small gifts that don't have a definite shape, such as earrings or handkerchiefs.
2) Draw two rectangles (each about an inch bigger than the width and length of your gift) on thick paper, with a half-inch flap on one side as shown.

3) Draw lines about half-inch long from the midpoints of the shorter side of each rectangle.
4) Draw a curve from the corners through the midpoint lines as shown.

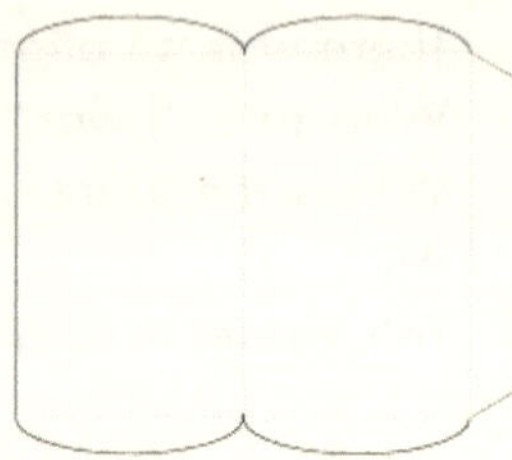

5) Score the midpoint lines hard with a knitting needle pointer the end of a paintbrush.
6) Cut the entire shape out.
7) Fold one rectangle over the other and paste one of the flaps down.
8) Now press on the long sides to form a tube, and fold in the short sides along the curved lines, until they spring into position producing a pillow shape.
9) Decorate the pillow with bits of paper, lace or sequins.
10) Push the gift into the pillow pack and close the flaps.

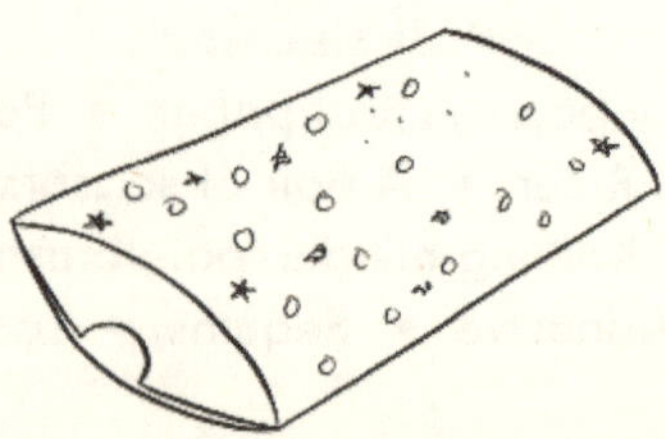

Milk Barfi

Make a lip-smacking sweet to put on your Rakhi plate

You need:

• Skimed-milk Powder 200 g • Reduced fat/fat free milk cream 225 g • Cardamom seeds powdered, 1/8 tsp • Sugar 100 g (to taste) • Preparation

PLEASE ASK A PARENT TO BE PRESENT AT ALL TIMES WHILE MAKING BARFIS.

MAKE IT!

1) Mix all the ingredients in a microwave safe deep bowl.
2) Put the bowl in a microwave for a total time of seven to eight minutes, switch off the microwave every two minutes and stir well.
3) Let the mixture cool for three to four minutes. Add sugar and mix well. Again put the bowl in the microwave for two minutes.
4) Take out the bowl and let it cool to a temperature that is comfortable to touch. Make a dough of the mixture and roll on a flat plate with a rolling pin or press by hand or with the bottom of a round bowl to a thickness of about five mm.
5) After two hours, cut the burfi in diamond or square shapes and serve!

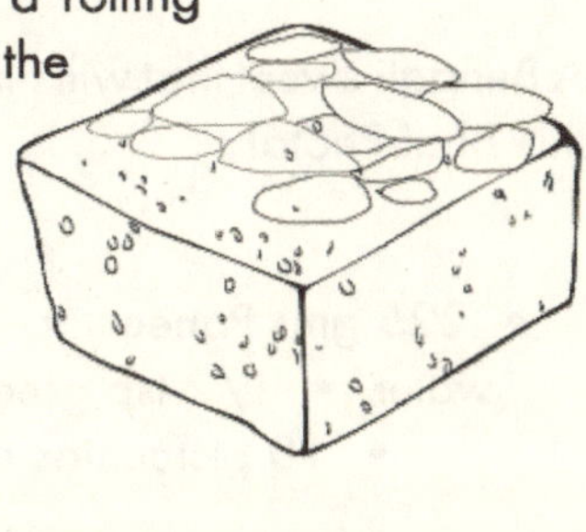

Make your own Mithai

One more great sweet idea to make your Rakhi delicious!

You need:

• Semolina (Sooji, Rava) 2 cups • Sugar 1 cup
• Ghee 2 tbs • Green Cardamom powder 1/2tbs
• Grated Coconut

PLEASE ASK A PARENT TO BE PRESENT AT ALL TIMES WHILE MAKING MITHAIS.

MAKE IT!

1) Heat ghee in the pan. Add semolina and fry it till it turns light brown. Keep aside.
2) Make some sugar syrup and add cardamom powder.
3) Put the pan on the fire again and add coconut and sugar syrup. Mix all the ingredients and stir it till it starts forming lumps. Cool it a little then put it in a tray or flat bowl, and make different shapes.

Sandesh

A Bengali sweet that will fill your sibling's heart with warmth, this Bhai Phota!

You need:

• 225 gms Paneer • 150 gms sugar • 1 tbsp rose water • 1/2 tsp green cardamom seeds (ground)
• 10 pistachios thinly sliced and crushed

PLEASE ASK A PARENT TO BE PRESENT AT ALL TIMES WHILE MAKING SANDESH.

MAKE IT!

1) Combine the sugar and paneer and mix well.
2) When the mixture solidifies, splash the rose water on it and remove the pan from the heat. Stir few more times.
3) Place the cardamom and pistachios in two separate plates.
4) Now divide the mixture into several portions of the required size and flatten them to give the desired shapes.
5) Dip each piece into both plates in turn so that the front of the sandesh is coated with crumbs.
6) Put into the fridge for two hours. Serve cold.

Family Tree

Give a gift to treasure, not just for your sibling, but for your whole family too!

You need:

- Passport size photographs of your whole family • Pen • Paper • Chart paper • Sketch pens and crayons

MAKE IT!

1) Write down the names of everyone in your family, starting from your grandparents.

2) Collect small passport size photographs from everyone in your family. If you can draw, draw small portraits of them.
3) First make a rough sketch of the family tree. Starting from the bottom, centre, write your and your sibling's names.
4) Now make a T above your names. On either side of the top of the T, write your parent's names. If your Dad has a sister, make a line next to his name, and write your aunt's name. Similarly do the same with your Mom's brother or sister.
5) Above your Dad's name, make another T and write your paternal grandparents' names. Repeat this with your mother's side. If you have a grand-aunt or grand-uncle, repeat the process from step 4.
6) Your basic tree should look something like this:

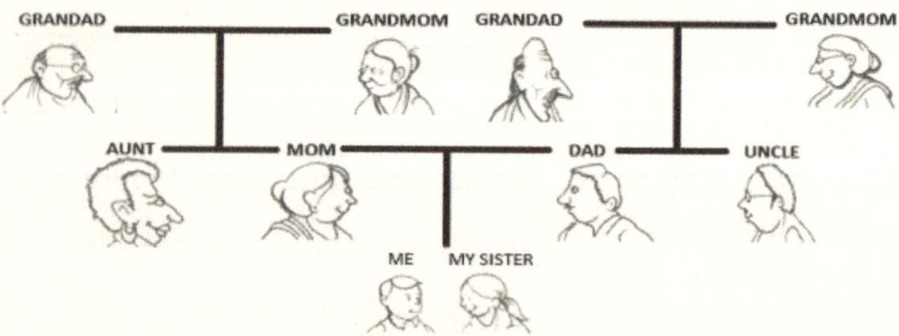

7) Draw this out on a chart, and paste the passport size photographs of all your family members under their names.
8) Now, on the chart paper, draw a tree, the bark right at the bottom. On top of the tree, on the green part, simply draw your family tree!

Festivals Rock!
Diary

Keep all your memoires of this year's Rakshabandhan and Bhai Dooj right here, in our special diary!

Everyone I gave a *rakhi* to, or got a *rakhi* from:

Everyone I celebrated Bhai Dooj with:

Everywhere I went this Rakhi and Bhai Dooj:

Everything I ate this Rakhi and Bhai Dooj:

All the gifts I gave this Rakhi and Bhai Dooj:

All the gifts I got, in return:

What I want to do next Rakhi and Bhai Dooj:

The most fun memory I have from this Rakhi and Bhai Dooj:

My favourite moment from this Rakhi and Bhai Dooj:

Draw your favourite moments from this year's festivities on the next two pages, or if you have photographs, paste them here:

Your Festival Playlist

Rakhi and Bhai Dooj Super Songlist!

'Phoolon Ka Taaron Ka'
Music Director: RD Burman
Singer: Kishore Kumar
From the film *Hare Rama Hare Krishna* (1971)

'Bhaiya Mere Raakhi Ke Bandhan Ko'
Music Directors: Shankar-Jaikishan
Singer: Lata Mangeshkar
From the film *Choti Behen* (1959)

'Behene Na Bhai'
Music Directors: Shankar-Jaikishan
Singer: Suman Kalyanpuri
From the film *Resham Ki Dori* (1974)

'Mere Bhaiya Mera Chandaa'
Music Director: Ravi
Singer: Asha Bhonsle
From the film *Kaajal* (1965)

'Chota Chota Bhaiyon Ke'
Music Director: Ram Lakshman
Singers: Kavita Krishnamurthy, Udit Narayan and Kumar Sanu
From the film *Hum Saath Saath Hai* (1999)

'Yeh Raakhi Bandhan Hai Aisa'
Music Directors: Shankar-Jaikishan
Singers: Lata Mangeshkar and Mukesh
From the film *Beimaan* (1972)

'Meri Behena'
Music Director: RD Burman
Singers: Kishore Kumar and Asha Bhonsle
From the film *Dhongree* (1979)

'Rang Birangi Rakhi Lekar'
Music Director: Madan Mohan
Singer: Lata Mangeshkar
From the film *Anpadh* (1962)

'Yeh Raksha Bandhan'
Music Director: Zameer Bikaneri
Singer: Preeti Sagar
From the film *Hum Bacchey Hindustan Ke* (1984)

'Hum Behenon Ke Liye'
Music Directors: Laxmikant-Pyarelal
Singer: Lata Mangeshkar
From the film *Anjaana* (1969)

Festival Movie Marathon!

Sachha Jhootha (1970)
Director: Manmohan Desai
Starring: Rajesh Khanna, Mumtaz and Vinod Khanna

Resham Ki Dori (1974)
Director: Atma Ram
Starring: Saira Banu and Dharmendra

Hare Rama Hare Krishna (1971)
Director: Dev Anand
Starring: Zeenat Aman, Dev Anand and Mumtaz

Josh (2000)
Director: Mansoor Khan
Starring: Shah Rukh Khan and Aishwarya Rai

Welcome (2007)
Director: Anees Bamzee
Starring: Akshay Kumar, Nana Patekar, Anil Kapoor and Katrina Kaif

Westside Story (1961)
Directors: Jerome Robbins, Robert Wise
Starring: Natalie Wood, George Chakiris and Richard Beymer

The Sound of Music (1965)
Director: Robert Wise
Starring: Julie Andrews, Christopher Plummer and Eleanor Parker

ET: The Extra-Terrestial (1982)
Director: Steven Speilberg
Starring: Henry Thomas, Drew Barrymore and Peter Coyote

Spy Kids (2001)
Director: Robert Rodriguez
Starring: Alexa Vega, Daryl Sabara and Antonio Banderas

The Incredibles (2004)
Director: Brad Bird
Starring: Craig T. Nelson, Samuel L. Jackson and Holly Hunter

Notes on the Contributors

Roopa Pai has won a Children's Book Trust Award for science writing. Among her published works are a four book science series—Science Sister (Pratham Books), and two girl power books, *Kaliyuga Sita* and *Mechanic Mumtaaz* (UNICEF). When she is not dreaming of plots for her stories, she goes on long bicycle rides, and takes children on history and nature walks in Bangalore.

Anu Kumar has held and given up several jobs but remained faithful to her first love, writing. Her books for children and young adults include *Atisa and the Seven Wonders* and *In the Country of Gold Digging Ants*, both published by Penguin/Puffin. She was awarded for her stories by the Commonwealth Broadcasting Association in 2004, and *The Little Magazine* in 2006. She has also written two novels for adults.

Rituparna Chatterjee lives a sci-fi life, thanks to her day job as a science and technology journalist in Silicon Valley. For play she transforms her discoveries into children's fiction and dreamy desserts. But that is only when she is not being followed by stray robot puppies obsessed with adopting her! Better known as the Purple Fairy of the Lost Woods, she arms children in the San Francisco Bay Area with floral chocolate wands and takes them on all kinds of adventures. Join the Purple Fairy on her adventures on www.readrituparna.com or on Twitter @ReadRituparna.

Deepa Agarwal has written more than 40 books for children and adults. *Caravan to Tibet* (Penguin/Puffin, 2007), selected for the Ibby Honour List 2008 as the best book from India, and a translation of the famous Hindi classic *Chandrakanta* (Penguin/Puffin, 2008) are two of her recent titles. Deepa has won the NCERT National Award for her picture book, *Ashok's New Friends* (Children's Book Trust). Five of her books have been listed in the White Raven Catalogue brought out by the IYL, Munich.

Ani Sengupta believes he is an animator who creates new characters and plays them in various settings. His young friends give him ideas of characters and incidents that he adds to his animation and together they make new stories. When Ani is not animating, he likes to visit scary places and play extreme sports like sky diving.

Kanika Sharma is a postgraduate in English Literature from Delhi University who has a penchant for Children's literature and folklore. Currently situated in Mumbai, she is working with Rupa Publications as a Freelance Editor. Finding the 'normal' world quite mundane, she often imagines a story is being told to her rather than the other way around. A mysterious presence with a flowing beard often accompanies her while she struggles with her broken pen.

Raja SG believes that children are true teachers for this World and his writings focus on delving into their creative minds. When he is not writing or working, he watches adventure movies and plays video games. Raja grew up in Mumbai and has travelled to many countries, using his travel experiences to write short stories with characters from different cultures and parts of the World.

Subhamoy Das is a former journalist and communications professional currently based in Hyderabad. He started writing for children's magazines as a teenager, contributing regularly for *Target*, *Teens Today*, *PCM Magazine* and *Children's Digest*. After completing his Master's degree in English Literature, he went on to study advertising and public relations at the Indian Institute of Mass Communication, New Delhi. He worked for several years as a journalist, illustrator and multimedia editor with India's leading media companies including the Hindustan Times Limited, the India Today Group and Cybermedia Limited. Since 1999, Subhamoy has been writing extensively on Hindu philosophy and Indian culture, for his popular blog hinduism.about.com, a top tier website owned by the New York Times Company.